ΤΟ ΘΑΝΑΤΙΚΟΝ ΤΗΣ ΡΟΔΟΥ

Καὶ τίς, ἠξεύρει νὰ μᾶς πῆ ὅλες τὲς τεχνοσύνες
τὰ κάμναν τὰ χειράκια τῶν καὶ τὲς ἐμορφοσύνες
Πλουμίδια καὶ πλντόφυλλα μὲ τέχνην καὶ μὲ τάξιν
ἐτίκνω εἰς ψιλὰ λινὰ λογιὲς ὀχρὲς μὲ τάξιν
Νὰ χρυσοκαββαρίζουσιν μπλάσμαν καὶ χρυσάφιν
μὲ πᾶσαν τέχνην μοσικήν ὡσὰν καλὸς ζωγράφος
Παρμπέρες, μαξελάρια, κουρτίνες καὶ μαντήλια,
μὲ κυδωνιὲς, τριανταφυλλιὲς, κλήματα καὶ σταφύλια
Ἄνθη καὶ ρόδα καὶ μυρτιὲς, πασί λογιά λουλούδια
μὲ πισθον νὰ πλουμίζουσιν, μὲ χαρὲς καὶ τραγούδια
Λέγω ἂν ἔτυχε κανεὶς νὰ τὰ καλοσκοπήση
Τἀργόχειρα τὰ κάμναλον, πολλὰ νάχεν θαυμάση

Embroidery
of the
Greek Islands
and Epirus

Embroidery
of the
Greek Islands
and Epirus

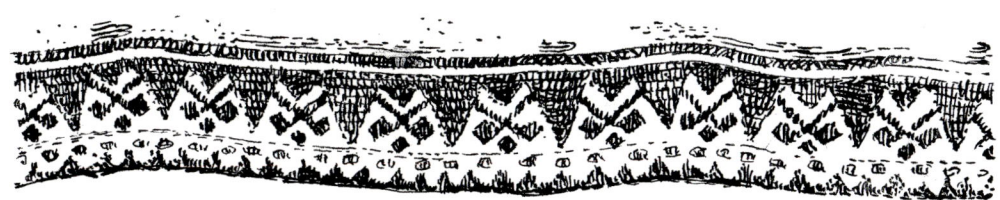

Roderick Taylor

with line drawings by Antony Maitland

INTERLINK BOOKS
An imprint of Interlink Publishing Group, Inc.
Brooklyn, N.Y.

MARSTON HOUSE • TAYLOR KERWIN LTD

First published in 1998
in the U.S. by
Interlink Books
An imprint of Interlink Publishing Group, Inc.
99 Seventh Avenue, Brooklyn, New York 11215

Library of Congress Cataloging-in-Publication Data
Taylor, Roderick.
    Embroidery of the Greek Islands / Roderick Taylor.
        p.   cm.
    Includes bibliographical references and index.
    ISBN 1-56656-289-9 (hardcover)
    1. Embroidery--Aegean Islands (Greece and Turkey)   I. Title
NK9251.A3A438 1998
746.4'4--dc21   98–12459
                                          CIP

First published in 1998
in the United Kingdom by
Marston House/Taylor Kerwin Ltd
Martson House, Marston Magna,
Yeovil, BA22 8DH

British Library Cataloguing-in-Publication Data
A catalogue record for this book is available from the British Library

ISBN 1 899296 05 0

Designed and produced by
Alphabet & Image Ltd, Marston House
Marston Magna, Yeovil, BA22 8DH, UK
Typeset by Remous, Milborne Port, Sherborne, Dorset
Printed and bound by Regent Publishing Services, Hong Kong

From that part of me which is Greek
R.R.T

Facing page: A cushion decorated with an Italian renaissance stylized flower. South Dodecanese, about 1800.

Frontispiece: Detail of a Cretan skirt border with a gorgon holding her double tail in a frieze of birds and flowers. Collected by Sandwith in 1879. Sphakia, before 1800. See page 108.

Contents

Foreword

Between 1650 and 1850 a number of small peasant communities in the Greek islands of the Aegean and the Adriatic produced a corpus of embroidery that is now recognised as one of the most spectacular and individual flowerings of this art. The islands have been fought over since neolithic times, progressing from being the centre of the civilized Greek world to being poor, isolated outposts of various empires that briefly controlled them before disappearing themselves.

The embroideries were the product of the native culture, fused with the cultures of all the nations that had conquered and settled or had passed through the area. The native Greek culture was based on that of the extended classical Greek world and on later manifestations of the Hellenistic world, mainly Greece, Coptic Egypt and Byzantium. The conquerors were the Franks and the Latins, Aragonese and Catalans, Venetians and Genoese and later the Ottomans. Some stayed longer than others and although some influenced the native Greeks and the way they lived, it was the conquerors themselves that were influenced by their stay and it was their lives that were changed.

The Crusaders were very attracted by the way of life that they had seen in the East and attempted to copy it during the three centuries of the Frankish rule in Greece. It was among the Norman, French and Italian families that formed the new nobility then resident in Greece that the Courteous Life was developed, and this affected the way it was to develop in Europe during the Middle Ages. Equally the way the Ottoman bureaucrats ran their empire was influenced by what they observed of the remnants of the Byzantine administration in the islands and in Anatolian Greece for three centuries before the Ottomans conquered Byzantium itself. Many of the faults in the Byzantine world that led to the fall of that empire were inherited by the Ottomans, and in turn led to the eventual fall of their empire. The virtues of both systems were, however, equally strong, first among them being the tolerance of other beliefs and the acceptance of other ways of living. Both empires had the ability not to overpower their new subjects by imposing a new culture on them, allowing them to pursue their own

The door to a set of bed curtains, two panels sewn at the single gable and open along the jambs, decorated with the double leaf and spitha pattern, highlit with dragons, dogs and goats with fat partridges set in the gable. Originally attributed to Patmos, but more likely south-western Cycladic, before 1750.

7

cultures once the formalities of paying allegiance and the various dues to the central authority had been observed.

In addition to these conquerors there were many waves of immigrants – the first were the Slavs and Albanians from the north; the Slavs before 1000 AD and the Albanians later. The Slavs were assumed to be fleeing from invaders from the east and the north and the Albanians were introduced by the Turks into Greece during one of their programmes of dislocating populations in order to reduce resistance to their rule. Later waves included various groups of European merchants and traders who established themselves in the area, making it the entre-pôt for trade with the East.

Various Italian Republics had been operating commercially in the area, principally in Constantinople since 1000 AD, and monks and pilgrims had been passing through on their way to the holy sites for three centuries before that. The Sephardic Jews arrived after their exile from Catholic Spain, settling in Salonika and throughout the northern provinces of Greece.

The British had established a consul for trade in Chios by 1513 and another in Crete by 1530. The Company of the Merchants of the Levant was established in 1581, predating the better known East India Company by three decades. The French king, Francis I, had signed a treaty with Sultan Soleiman in 1536, and the Dutch had consuls in the Aegean from the beginning of the sixteenth century. During the Venetian occupation the Italians brought with them large communities of Catholic priests and nuns that set up convents and schools, creating a class of educated craftsmen and merchants.

Finally, following the Ottoman series of conquests and reconquests, a new administration and bureaucracy was installed in the islands, composed of peoples from all over the Ottoman Empire, among them Slavs, Moroccans, Egyptians, Armenians and Jews. The islands also became a favourite place for exiles from the court at Istanbul, who brought with them small communities of friends and introduced the manners and style of the metropolis.

The result of all this movement and the introduction of foreign ideas was the creation of a new local tradition of craft and folklore, which included a wealth of individual and distinctive embroideries. These are now justly considered to be of great artistic significance and have been avidly collected for over a hundred years, gradually being concentrated in a number of museums, mainly through donations and bequests.

This book is limited to those embroideries produced in the Greek islands of the Aegean and the Ionian Seas and in Epirus, and draws on the main museum collections and on as many private ones as possible. It will attempt to study the total field rather than a single collection. I do not attempt to discuss the total corpus of Greek embroidery: obviously a great deal was made – every girl worked on her trousseau and all women worked with the needle in the little spare time they had; their production inevitably covers every degree of skill and invention and much of it does not warrant being even considered.

Most of it was decorated for daily use and was not intended to last for more than the maker's lifetime. I shall concentrate on those pieces that show the greatest invention and which exemplify the work as a whole. These are the pieces that were treasured when they were made and have, consequently, survived today. My interest is in the domestic textiles and I will only refer to church vestments and costume when they are relevant to an understanding of the other work.

I owe an enormous debt to those who, at a time when such a domestic craft was not considered as art and not worth collecting, did collect, and clearly spent considerable time and effort in finding and saving these pieces. Their fate otherwise would have been that of so many pieces that were consigned to the rubbish heaps or to the dealers who cut them up and sold them as recycled tourist trash.

I also owe a great debt to the curators of the various museums that first studied and wrote about their collections, particularly to Alan John Bayard Wace, who was both a collector and a curator, and to Pauline Johnstone, a successor to Wace at the Victoria & Albert Museum, who wrote the first book I ever saw on these textiles. I had started to collect textiles without knowing anything about them and before I had ever seen a book on them, but the passion was quick and took deeply. I am particularly indebted to the Trustees and the Decorative Arts Curator of the National Museums and Galleries on Merseyside, Liverpool Museum, for their kind permission to reproduce for the first time a large number of textiles from the Wace Collection.

I would like to thank all the museum curators and the collectors who very kindly answered all my questions, even if they were sometimes very detailed and required considerable research. I am also very grateful to all those who have very kindly provided me with photographs of all the pieces that I did not get to see myself, although I have seen and studied the vast majority of pieces described or referred to in this book.

The corner of a cover decorated with a mythical bird-deer with long tined horns alternating with geometric plant forms. Cycladic, either Anafi or Ios, before 1800.

1   *The Historical Background*

In ancient Greece the Aegean was seen as the centre of Hellas with greater Greece surrounding it on all four sides, and Delos was the geographic and emotional centre of that world. From then until the Fourth Crusade in 1204, when our specific interest in these islands can be said to start, they had become isolated, growing less and less important in the Greek world. They were one of the administrative Themes of the Byzantine Empire, the Karavisianon, which included all the islands in the Aegean except the Northern Sporades, which belonged to the Theme of Salonika. The Byzantines were able to administer the mainland Themes but they slowly lost control of the islands. They over-taxed them when they could but otherwise they abandoned them to the pirates, to the Arabs and Turks who occasionally attacked them, and to the petty local chieftains that arose from time to time. The islands were subjected to the slow incursions of the merchant adventurers from the new commercial City States of Italy that gradually extended their activities to the east, following in the steps of pilgrims and crusaders.

Eventually the Byzantines abandoned control of the Aegean, as they were to lose it in mainland Greece and Turkey. They sold trading privileges to the Italian republics, formalising the existing activities of their merchants. They signed an agreement with Venice as early as 1020, with the Republic of Amalfi in 1056, with Genoa in 1098 and with the Pisans in 1110. All these foreigners were extremely competitive with each other, bringing into their business activities the political rivalries current in Italy.

The islands produced many products that the expanding Italian and European markets required: linen, cotton, cereals, wine and, above all, silk. The islands were also very important stops on the pilgrim routes - the Venetians held this profitable Christian tourist industry as a virtual monopoly and this activity attracted Mediterranean pirates to set up in the islands. Even the Venetians operated as opportunistic pirates, attacking any vessel that was not Venetian, including those carrying pilgrims.

A portolano by Georgios Sideris. This pilot's chart was made about 1600 but still shows a Genoese flag covering Chios and the Hospitallers' cross on Rhodes, although both had fallen to the Ottomans about a hundred years earlier. Wind-stars are placed all over, showing the wind directions. Egg tempera on vellum.

In their need to secure safe harbours in the islands the new powers were responsible for more development in the area than the Byzantines had carried out in the previous eight hundred years. During the two hundred years after the Venetians had been granted trading privileges the other republics, particularly the Genoese, infiltrated the eastern islands of Rhodes and Chios, where they set up regular commercial activities. The Genoese set up their first headquarters as pirates in Melos before consolidating their position in Chios, and they even spread into the Black Sea, establishing trading posts on the shores of the Caucasus from where they imported the silk that was destined for the new looms of Lucca and Genoa. All this movement in the area, and the Venetian reaction to this new competition, must be seen as one of the principal causes of the shameful episode of the Fourth Crusade.

The Venetians undertook to supply vessels, men-at-arms, horses and provisions for the Crusade, which had intended to go directly to the Holy Land. Because the French organisers couldn't raise the money the Venetians agreed to continue with the venture, everything being all prepared, on condition that the Fleet would first subdue a Venetian colony, Zara, on the Dalmatian coast, that was trying to break away. That done, the crusaders were persuaded to help the exiled Byzantine emperor, Alexius Alexander, regain the throne. Alexius had been in Venice, and in return for this help was prepared to offer the Venetians special trading rights. The emperor also undertook to submit the Eastern Orthodox Church to the Church in Rome, extending the Latin Rite throughout the Byzantine Empire and, in addition, to pay the Venetians 200,000 marks for their help.

After their arrival in Byzantium in June 1203 the crusaders took the city and placed Alexius Alexander on the throne, but he was murdered before he could honour any of his commitments to his Venetian allies. He was replaced by Murtzuphlos, a Byzantine general who had made no agreement with the Venetians and was certainly not prepared to accept the imposition of the Latin Rite in the empire. The Venetians realised that their venture was foundering and so on 12 April 1204, under the direct order of the Doge, Enrico Dandolo, they stormed Byzantium from within, destroying and sacking the city for three days. They looted its inheritance of accumulated wealth, especially the sacred relics and priceless reliquaries, which they sent back to Venice. They persecuted the Orthodox clerics and congregation and imposed the Latin Rite on the Church. They then shared out the empire. A quarter became the Latin Empire of Romania with Baldwin, Count of Flanders, as emperor. The remainder was divided in two: the Venetians took half for themselves while the other half was distributed, piecemeal, to members of the conquering army that had started out as a crusade to liberate Jerusalem from the Infidels.

Thus was created the Frankish Empire of Greece, with Kings of Salonika, Princes of Achaia, Despots of Epirus, Megaskyrs of Athens and Dukes of the Archipelago. Constantinople itself was placed under the control of the catholic Baldwin who was made Emperor of the

Detail of a Cretan skirt border showing rows of sea monsters, dragons and nereids, with a central harpy above the border of a leafy vine rising from a square pot. Crete, before 1700.

Latin East. This action immediately caused those parts of the empire that would not accept Frankish rule and that wished to maintain the Orthodox Rite to break off into independent empires.

It was this appalling conquest and partitioning of the empire that, by weakening its structure, is said to have led to the eventual conquest of Constantinople by the Ottomans in 1453, although it would be wrong to suggest that it was the sole cause. The sack of Byzantium was the beginning of a dramatic change in the Aegean, and the native culture was suddenly overlaid with a foreign, technologically more advanced, one.

Seventeen of the islands of the Aegean, those known today as the Cyclades, plus Astypalaia, were created the Duchy of the Archipelago. The first Duke was Marco Sanudo, a nephew of the Doge Enrico Dandolo who had instigated the sack of Constantinople. He first had to take the islands from the Genoese, who were established there as pirates. The Sanudo family ruled as Dukes from 1207 to 1383, when Francesco Crispi, a son-in-law of a later Duke, had Nicolo II assassinated and took over the Duchy himself. The Crispi then held the Duchy until 1566 when the Turks conquered the majority of the islands.

Between 1566 and 1579 the Duchy survived as an independent state, consisting of Naxos, Paros and Melos, and ruled by Joseph Nasi. Nasi was by origin a Portuguese Jew who had fled to Istanbul, been converted to Islam and become a favourite of the Sultan Selim II, known to posterity as The Sot. Selim gave Nasi the Duchy to exploit commercially, on condition that he paid an annual tribute to his patron at the Sublime Porte. It seems that Nasi never even visited the islands of which he was the ruler when he cast ambitious eyes on Cyprus, which he hoped to rule as Duke, providing Selim with the Cypriot wine he so loved. The project fell through when Selim died in 1574 and Nasi disappears from history soon after that. The Duchy finally disintegrated and only Tinos remained in Venetian hands, until it too was taken by the Ottomans in 1712.

The Latin Empire of the East, under the Emperors Baldwin I and II, lasted only fifty years, until 1261, when the Orthodox emperor, Michael VIII Paleologus, returned to his capital, which was virtually all that remained of the empire. The only Franks who stayed in Constantinople were the merchants and a few clerics. In the islands, however, particularly in the Cyclades, a two-layered system of society developed where the Italian Latin Rite families owned the land and governed the indigenous Greek Orthodox population, with the urban population remaining separated from the rural one. This system made it quite possible for the larger rural population not to be affected by the conquest, preserving their language, church and culture away from the urban centres.

The history of the Dodecanese and the eastern Aegean Islands is different to that of the western Aegean Islands. Although the members of the crusade were apportioned all the islands of the Aegean under their agreement with the Latin kingdom, which would have included the Dodecanese, they were never able to impose control on them. They were left to the invading Turks, the pirates and to the Genoese, who slowly spread there after losing their hold in the Cyclades.

Chios was given under a renewable lease to the Genoese Benedetto Zaccaria in 1262 by the Emperor Michael VIII, as prepayment for the Genoese agreement to fight against the Venetians. The Genoese held Chios under successive leases from the emperors of Byzantium until 1329, when they were forced to leave, and Chios reverted to being part of the Byzantine Empire until 1346. At that date the Giustiniani of Genoa took over the island and controlled it as a Limited Company issuing shares, the Mahona, and virtually all the shareholders, the Mahonesi, took the name and arms of the Giustiniani family, and were known by such names as Giustiniani quondam Geronimo, Giustiniani quondam Ottoviano. They ran the island as a commercial enterprise exporting wine, cotton, silk woven fabrics and the mastic of which Chios was the only producer. They introduced an industrial society which was similar to that being established in Genoa. When the Ottomans, under a renegade Hungarian admiral, Piali Pasha, took Chios in 1566, they inherited the first industrial society in the Ottoman Empire, with textiles as the main product. The grander Imperial textiles were still being made traditionally by hand in Istanbul and Bursa. The first machinery for textile production, ginning and weaving, was introduced by the Genoese into Chios, not only contributing to the wealth of the island but also enriching the language with the Italian words for the machines, the processes and the final products.

Rhodes and the Southern Sporades, as the Dodecanese were called, formed part of the Sea Theme of Karavisianon within the Byzantine Empire, and were commanded by an admiral, the Drungarius. Between 1204 and 1250 they were ruled by the Cretan Gabalas family, who were replaced by a Genoese family, the de'Vignoli, who later agreed to house the Knights of St John in Rhodes, if they would help him evict the Turks who had conquered parts of Rhodes and the other islands. The Knights had been defeated in the Holy Land and ousted from Jerusalem and had been unable to settle in Cyprus, so Rhodes, with its splendid natural harbour and its importance as a staging point on the pilgrim route, was an ideal new centre for them. Under their newly elected Master, Fulk de Villaret, they agreed to de'Vignoli's terms and in 1310 set out to conquer Rhodes, which they were to share. The agreement somehow soured and the Templars acquired Rhodes and the de'Vignoli disappeared from the scene. Two years after this conquest the Order of the Templars was dissolved by Pope John XX11 and the Hospitallers inherited all the wealth and possessions of the Templars.

By 1340 the Knights had conquered the Dodecanese as far north as Patmos and Lipsos, making Kos into their second centre, but never took Karpathos and Kasos in the south, which remained under Venetian control until taken by the Turks in 1572. The Knights held Rhodes and the surrounding islands until 1522 when the Sultan, Soleiman the Magnificent, conquered the island. He allowed the new Master, Villiers de l'Isle Adam, to leave the island on the 1st January 1523 in great dignity, taking with him whatever of the Order's possessions he wished, with as many of the inhabitants as wanted to seek a new centre with him. Not only was Soleiman magnanimous in his behaviour but unlike other conquerors he did not then set out to remove all traces of the Knights and their occupation; many of the Hospitaller monuments still exist on the islands, even if they have been later restored.

The influence of the Knights in the Dodecanese was as strong as that of the Venetians in the Cyclades. In a sense it was stronger, because in the Cyclades the numbers of the Latins were relatively small, and their Catholicism kept them apart from the local inhabitants, whereas in the

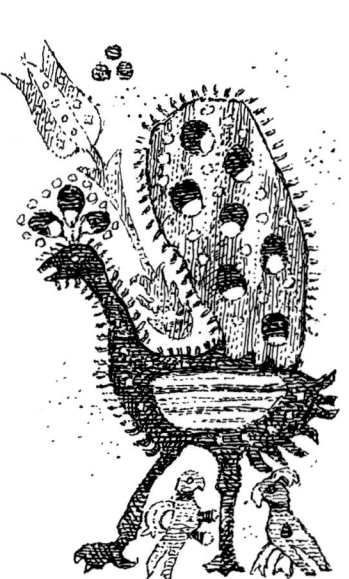

Dodecanese the number of the Knights and their entourages, which included the Gasmouli, children of the Latins and local Greeks and Turks, was much greater in relation to the total population and their religion did not keep them as apart.

The Knights, as they slowly declined from being the 'Servants of the Poor' to being masters of the sea, introduced a style of life that was that of the luxury-loving patrician society of Europe rather than that of the ascetic monk. They sought power on the sea fighting against Turks, Mamluks and the pirates, and occasionally acting as pirates themselves. They also introduced into the islands a new culture, which embraced architecture, both military and domestic, literature and the craft of textile production, which included embroidery. In 1685 the Venetians, under Morosini, started a new campaign to wrest the area back from the Turks, particularly to regain Crete, the flower of their island empire. The reconquest was short-lived and by 1712 the area was once again under Turkish dominion.

The Ottomans ruled the Aegean from the middle of the sixteenth century until the middle of the nineteenth. The islands always remained isolated both from the rest of the Ottoman Empire, and from the social and political changes that were taking place in Europe. The Ottoman influence was slow to develop, emanating from Istanbul and then percolating through to the provincial islands of the Great White Sea, which was the conventional Turkish name for the western seas. The influence was one of manners and custom, and like the Franks before them they influenced a part of the urban society but were less able to change the rural population. They, once more, maintained their language, religion and culture despite the new conquerors. The areas most influenced by the Ottoman Turks were Skyros and the Sporades and the islands near the Turkish coast, including Chios.

Chios became the main importing centre for most European products destined for the Ottoman Empire after the final defeat of the Venetians in 1715. Chios was on the main trade routes, unlike Istanbul which was the end of a run. It was from Chios that one went to the other islands and to Syria and Egypt. Also the problems that Istanbul presented in terms of bureaucracy, customs charges and the heavy expenditure in 'gifts' were avoided by shipping through Chios, where the duties on textiles were less, and where export rebates and free port facilities were available.

The English had established a consul in Chios for the Ottoman Empire and the Aegean in 1513, although they had been trading with the Turks since the middle of the fifteenth century. They exported English cloth, such as kersies, worsteds and hollands; Rycaut mentions that at the beginning of the seventeenth century the soldiers of the Turkish army were dressed in red English cloth.

The Levant Company of Turkey Merchants existed from 1581 until 1825, when it surrendered all the grants, privileges and immunities that it had held, because the Napoleonic wars, the growth of industry in western Europe and the disintegration of the Ottoman Empire had

Detail from a curtain border, decorated with a repeat of two peacocks set about a standing flower within a twisted ribbon of an 'S' and a stylized carnation. The design is derived from Mamluk embroidery. Siphnos, about 1800.

made the venture less profitable. The Company had paid the costs of the British Ambassador to the Sublime Porte until 1803, when the British government took over that expense, receiving in exchange the consulates and the embassy premises in Istanbul which had been originally granted to and financed by the Levant Company.

The history of both Crete and the Province of Epirus is very different to that of the other islands, and will be recounted in the introduction to each section.

The Ionian Islands, like the Aegean Islands, were very important links in the development of trade between Italy and the East. During the Byzantine rule of the islands Corfu formed the bulwark of the Byzantine Empire to the west and was continuously under attack by the Italians. Even at that time the Venetians used it as part of their trade chain, which stretched from Zara to the western coast of the Caucasus and to the mouth of the Nile. The Ionian islands changed hands many times, belonging to Epirus, Naples and Venice and even to the Roman Orsini under the Angevins.

After the Greek War of Independence in 1821-22 the Ottoman hold on the area started to disintegrate and the New Greece was created in 1832, consisting of the Morea, the mainland as far north as the Gulf of Volos, Euboea, the Cyclades and the Sporades. The Ionian Islands were ceded to the new state by the British in 1864. Thessaly was annexed in 1881, Macedonia, Crete and the eastern Aegean Islands were taken by Greece as the result of the Balkan Wars in 1912-13, Thrace was added in 1922-23, and finally Rhodes and the Dodecanese were ceded by Italy to Greece in 1947.

2   *Cultural Influences*

The embroideries of the Greek islands show clearly the effect of the various influences to which the whole area had been exposed over the centuries. That of ancient Greece is not apparent in the designs themselves, but is evident in the way that the structure and plan of the houses and their internal arrangement have affected the type of textiles that were made and how they were used.

The ground plan of a classical-period village would differ very slightly from that of a medieval one, which would certainly have been built on the footings of the earlier site. The house structure, which earlier only had external walls and where internal divisions were made by the use of curtains, *peripetasmata* (a word no longer used), persisted up to the introduction of new building materials during the nineteenth century. The ancient designs with which modern embroideries and textiles are decorated are part of the classical revival that started with Schliemann's discoveries in Mycenae and Troy. They renewed interest in the ancient world and old patterns became suddenly fashionable and were incorporated into contemporary design. They are not part of a continuous, uninterrupted tradition.

The earliest enduring influence is Byzantium, which was itself subject to all the influences of the Near and Far East, acquiring the use of the basic materials and the techniques of weaving from the classical world and also from China, the Sassanian Empire and Egypt. The technique of embroidery, although it is thought to have its origin in China, in fact arrived in the Aegean via Rome and the Roman Empire, and was later developed further during the period of prolonged contact with Renaissance Italy.

The main Byzantine influence can be discerned in the repertory of designs, many of which are religious and allegorical. They include the vase between opposed animals, a range of heraldic and symbolic animals, floral patterns based on the decorated borders found in mosaics, pairs of trees and small architectural features such as fountains and door portals. It is also strongly discernible in the traditional shape and cut of women's dresses, particularly the shift dress, *poukamiso*.

Detail from an Epirote wedding bolster (see page 135), showing the mounted best man in Turkish dress, wearing a turban. Yanina, about 1700.

19

Byzantium ruled primarily through its Civil Service, which was very closely tied to the administration of the Orthodox Church. A large number of ecclesiastical and liturgical garments have survived but their patterns are as often those of Renaissance Italy as they are of Byzantium. A large number of vestments, mainly copes and altar frontals, made from re-cycled domestic textiles, have survived from isolated communities in the Aegean. Many very impressive embroidered liturgical cloths have also survived but these are all professional products of the Great City. Virtually no secular garments of the Byzantine or Latin Empire period have survived, although Byzantium did supply all Christian Europe with superb textiles, some fragments of which have been re-used in liturgical and funerary garments, and which remain as a testimony to the magnificence of the industry from the sixth to the fifteenth centuries.

The second influence is that of the Mamluks, who were the inheritors of part of the Byzantine Empire of the East. The Mamluks were not a maritime people, even though their empire did encircle the eastern Mediterranean. They depended on the islands of the Aegean and their current lords to provide them with vessels and crews. The trade between the islands and the Mamluk world was important and

Above A long scarf decorated with a domed and arcaded Orthodox Church and two side-chapels showing the interiors with hanging lamps. The figures above the church must be a bride and groom with a best man. The scarf would have been donated to the church and used there as an icon cloth. Skyros, before 1800.

Right A Mamluk sampler showing a range of border patterns used in Fatimid and Mamluk embroidery and weaving. These patterns were used widely in Cycladic and Dodecanese embroidery. Cairo, fifteenth century.

the Venetians, together with the other trading Italian republics, throughout the whole period traded directly with Egypt and Syria, and from their outposts in the islands made contact with the Arab world. This continuous contact made the movement of designs and styles very simple: patterns that came from Egypt passed through the Greek islands and moved west to become established in Italy and then throughout Europe. The same designs and the way to use them were absorbed by the Ottomans into their textile traditions and moved east into that empire, and even into the Ottoman territories in North Africa.

The Mamluk world inherited the skills and crafts of the Pharaonic world, which included the textile skills of that culture and of the Graeco-Roman culture that followed it. A substantial part of the Cycladic repertory of pattern and design can be traced to the Mamluk world; this point has been made many times before but perhaps the extent of the influence has not been emphasised sufficiently. The two

great patterns – the branch, *spitha*, with the enclosed birds and dogs, and the large leaf pattern, *bradyfyllo* – which are the backbone of so much island pattern, are both derived from Mamluk originals. Many other smaller motifs, such as the dog, the long-eared rabbit, the star-shaped medallions and the shrub in a pot can also be traced to Mamluk textiles.

p.6

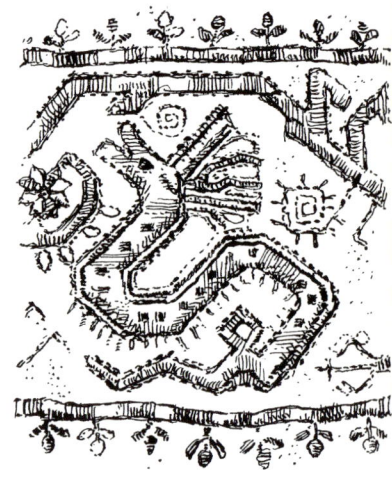

The influence from Mamluk art can be seen even more strongly in the larger overall designs and in the placing of patterns within the structure. Although relatively little domestic embroidery has survived from the great period of Mamluk art, a number of small embroidery samplers have survived. These show a range of running patterns that appear in the island work and also in many European pieces of the fourteenth and fifteenth centuries. These are the bands composed of geometric patterns developed within the Islamic tradition of art. They include the bands of formalised tendrils, the alternating motifs contained in cartouches, the trellis composed of diagonal rhomboids and the small swastika and 'S' motifs. Many of the motifs associated with the Ottoman repertory can first be seen in Graeco-Roman textiles and in the Mamluk work produced within the Tiraz system. The embroideries of the Maghreb and Moorish Spain also use the same repertory, which they received directly from the same source, either through the initial Arab conquest and occupation, or later through the administration of the Ottoman Empire.

The third influence is that of the Frankish and Venetian occupation, which introduced into the islands patterns from the west. These were derived from all the textile arts, many arriving via the embroidery and lace pattern books that were newly being printed in Italy. Editions such as Giovanni Antonio Tagliente's *Essempio di Recammi* of 1524, Tommaso Gazzoni's *La Piazza Universale* of 1585 and Cesare Vecellio's *Corona delle Donne* of 1591, were among the first to formalise the tradition of patterns that had been used and passed down within communities for centuries.

In addition to these linear patterns, such as the complex Naxian geometric ones, there is a range of western European designs, such as the mermaid with the divided tail and adapted heraldic birds and lions, to be found in both Cretan and Sporadic textiles. The range of mythical beasts found in Astypalaian textiles is reminiscent of the late medieval Perugia towels, Buratto lace from Venice and the Andaluz fabrics of Mudejar Spain.

p.48, 49

p. 13, 109

p.55, 78

The Frankish and later Italian rule of the islands also introduced into the area new styles and the use of articles common in the more sophisticated western world. It would be excessive to say that they introduced the use of the bed as a permanent fixture of the house, but they certainly made the use more popular and gave it a new importance. The greatest pieces of island interior decoration were made to be used with the bed, as fits a new departure in style.

The final influence on the area, and a strong one in certain of the islands, particularly the Sporades, was that of the Ottomans. This last

influence overlays the others, arriving at the time of greatest growth in the islands, the stabilising of the political situation and the availability of the technical means of production. The islands were part of the Ottoman Empire from 1522, when they were known as the Admiralate of the Great White Sea, until the War of Independence in 1822, when they were incorporated into the New Greece.

The influence of the Ottomans was slow to develop. Fashion and style invariably started in Istanbul and then percolated through to the provinces, carried there by the expatriate administrators. The influence was one of manners and custom, and like the Franks before them they only influenced a part of the urban society and were less able to influence the rural populations, which once more maintained their religion, language and culture, despite the new conquerors. The areas most influenced by the Ottomans were Skyros and the islands near the Turkish coast, Chios and Crete.

The combination of these four influences - Byzantium, the Italian-Frankish Empire of Greece, Mamluk Egypt and finally the Ottomans - can be observed most clearly in the embroideries of the Aegean, where the overlays of inspiration and the repertory of designs have together created the world of these marvellous textiles.

A skirt border worked in an Italian renaissance style of a repeated pattern set in a wide border, edged top and bottom with two alternating motifs, giving the effect of punto in aria work. The main motif is the double-headed eagle set in a black and white wrought-iron shape. Again spaces are filled with pairs of mannikins, hares and birds. Crete, about 1750.

23

3 *Introduction to the Textiles*

Greek embroidery can be divided into two main groups: mainland Greece and the islands. Mainland embroidery is almost exclusively associated with women's costume, whereas that of the islands is primarily associated with the decorating of the house, which was usually a single room, sometimes sub-divided.

Mainland costume embroidery forms part of the larger corpus of Balkan embroidery and is best studied as part of that subject. The exception is Epirus which, because of its different history and the strength of its native culture, produced a large body of work that shares a tradition with the islands and has usually, as here, been studied with those embroideries. Epirote costume embroideries, as with those of neighbouring Thrace and Macedonia, remain part of the Balkan tradition.

All the embroidery made in the Greek islands has so far been treated as if it were one homogenous tradition. This is clearly neither true nor satisfactory and a more detailed classification is necessary. In this book I have separated the embroideries into these main groupings:

Cyclades

south-western:	Pholegandros, Melos and Kimolos
south-eastern:	Amorgos, Anafi, Ios and Astypalaia
central:	Naxos, Paros and Siphnos

Dodecanese

central:	Rhodes
northern:	Kos, Nisyros, Kalymnos, Patmos and Astypalaia
south-western:	Karpathos and Kasos

Sporades	Skyros and Skiathos
Northern Islands	Chios, Mytiline, Samothrace and Thasos
Crete	
Ionian Islands	Corfu, Paxos, Levkas, Cephalonia, Ithaka and Zakinthos
Epirus	

Far left A panel from a set of bed curtains showing three columns of alternating broad-leaf and spitha set within a border of a Mamluk pattern with inset dogs. Cycladic, before 1720. *Left* A panel from a set of bed curtains showing a central column of an adapted spitha pattern with peacocks, and a broad panel of the same pattern at the base. Each panel is flanked with a rising border composed of diamonds set with little dogs and geometric patterns. South Cycladic, before 1700.

I have found no certain, irrefutable way of attributing the various types of embroidery to specific islands. It is certainly not possible to do so either by analysing the materials or the repertory of stitches used in making them. Linen, cotton and silk were all used throughout the area and the stitches, with a very few exceptions, were common to all the islands. A study of the social history of the area and the way in which the various embroidered pieces were used, combined with an analysis of the patterns and the way in which they appear to have developed, has allowed me to make certain suggestions about the provenance of the embroideries. These are, however, only considered suggestions and if more information does become available, I will be delighted to change my attributions in the face of solid proof.

Certain names have become accepted for various groups of Greek embroidery, usually because of an initial arbitrary decision on the part of a collector or a dealer. It is only with caution that one should attempt to attribute embroideries to groups of islands, much less to particular villages in specific islands. Pieces such as the well documented and very characteristic embroideries from Naxos were copied and worked in the neighbouring islands of Paros and Antiparos, and the Naxos style certainly influenced the work done in Skyros and even in islands as far away as Thasos in the northern Aegean. p.104 Attributions to Naxos must therefore include both embroideries made in Naxos and those in the Naxos style made elsewhere. In the same p.48, 49, 93 way the Rhodian style of embroidery and patterns were certainly copied in Tilos and Symi, which are both near, but also in Karpathos, Kasos and Castellorizo, which are not. So, even in discussing a piece with an ostensible provenance one must be aware that it may, in fact, have come from elsewhere.

Styles and designs moved about the area, either through commerce or through the more traditional process of marriages between island families, where the new bride brought her dowry embroidered with patterns of her native island with her. In time her daughter would copy these inherited patterns into her own embroidery, combining the new motifs with local ones, making it no longer possible to say that because a piece has this motif or is set out in such a way that it must therefore have come from one particular island or village. However, in order to have some frame of reference it is necessary to describe pieces by an accepted island name, acknowledging that the name identifies a type rather than a certain provenance; where I have no reason to suggest an alternative name I have retained the accepted one.

The historical references that do exist are from accounts left by travellers - Pietro Casola on pilgrimage to the Holy Land in 1494 says that there were available in the markets of Rhodes: 'so many cloths of every make, tapestry, brocades and hangings of every design, carpets of every sort, camlets of every colour and texture, silks of every kind.' Pierre Belon, who was in Rhodes about 1550, which was thirty years after the Knights had been ousted from the island, mentions that women were embroidering those bed tents that are still the main article

of Rhodian embroidery. He says: '*L'on trouve a acheter de beaux ouvrages de soye faits a l'éguille, et principalement des pavillions de licts. Ils font leurs ouvrages en diverse couleurs en manières de poincts croisez. Le portraict est de feuillage et est different a l'ouvrage Tourquois, et a celui qui est faict a Chio et en Chypre.*' In his *Livre des Singularitées Observées* of 1555 he also mentions that Jewish women act as middle-men selling needlework in the markets, for they are allowed to go about uncovered; they sell napkins, handkerchiefs, sashes, cushion covers, and works of greater value such as bed tents in various fashions. Not many pieces survive from this period, although it is very likely that later pieces do not differ greatly from those produced then.

The literary evidence is more immediate, stemming as it does from

p.37
p.56, 58 60

the same period and environment as the fabrics. The charming lines from *The Plague at Rhodes* by Emmanuel Georgillas, written in 1485, which is quoted in full at the start of this book, shows that the art of embroidery, although well established, was both taken for granted and under-valued even then. In the collection of *45 Stories from the Dodekanese*, make by Jacob Zarraftis, dating from the seventeenth and eighteenth centuries, edited by Professor Dawkins in 1953, the tale of Yavrouda starts with a description of a teacher of embroidery and gives a list of all the articles that she teaches her pupils to embroider. If these tales are from the beginning of the eighteenth century, then it is evident that the tradition continued in the same form even under the Ottoman occupation.

The collectors provide the next link in the process of attributing the embroideries. They occasionally mention where they bought a piece and then attribute the piece to that place, even if the piece itself denies that likelihood. The majority of accepted attributions are derived from the names given by the collectors, principally Wace, who was collecting before 1905 and who had no existing names on which to base his finds. It is he who organised the first exhibition of these textiles at the Fitzwilliam Museum in Cambridge in 1906, and he was also the first to publish on the embroideries, these later publications adding authority to his initial attributions.

The habit of naming pieces from their point of purchase is old and powerful. The best example of this is the case of the embroidered quilt covers which were first purchased by westerners in Rhodes. They were always attributed to Rhodes and identified as products of the Knights' tenure of the island, both because of the sophistication of the work and for the romantic associations of that period. We now know that they

Two borders from Cretan skirts. These early examples used Italian patterns which were published and circulating from about 1500. The work is European but the provincial origin is given away by the little intrusive birds in the blue skirt. Collected by Sandwith in 1879.

28

were made in Istanbul, Epirus, Skyros, and almost certainly in many large towns in the Ottoman Empire, and it is likely that none were made in Rhodes at all. It was the standard practice that all Greek island pieces offered for sale right up to the beginning of the 1914 war were classified as either Rhodes or Yanina work. The catalogue of Greek island embroideries in the Dresden Museum, which had been collected before 1887, calls them Rhodian, although they are quite obviously Naxian. This happens throughout the textile world and persists wherever the fiction is pleasing or romantic and commercially advantageous.

The first problem to be confronted is what to call the whole corpus of work. It is generally accepted and sensible that they be called Greek island work. However, at the time of their production the islands were part of the Latin or Venetian empires and later of the Ottoman Empire. Furthermore, the embroideries were made by all the inhabitants, be they Greeks, Franks or Italians, Jews or Turks.

If attributions are confusing then dating the fabrics presents a whole new world of problems. Other than a few Cretan skirts which are dated, there are no dates on the textiles. As traditions and techniques did not change for generations dating becomes contentious; at most one can derive relative dating information from the developments of patterns and on the use of different ground cloths and new colours. But this, at most, only allows one to state that one piece may be older than another. The earliest dated Cretan skirt is 1697, others range between 1726 and 1762 and one can assume that they were made both before and after these dates. The oldest of the embroideries that have survived, those from the Cyclades, give the appearance of being from the middle of the seventeenth century. I can see neither reason nor proof for dating any piece earlier than that. Visitors to the islands from as early as 1750 mention that although the women still wear the traditional embroidered dresses they no longer make them, and that the pieces of domestic embroidery that were still held in houses were treated as precious heirlooms, only being brought out to be admired or to be used as display pieces for special occasions.

p.77, 80, 81

It is obvious that embroidery made in the nineteenth century was not of the quality of the earlier pieces, either in design or in execution. It is not until the craft was revived in the early twentieth century that a new higher standard of technique and quality was reintroduced.

The eventual demand for tourist souvenirs changed the revived domestic craft of embroidery into a new industry with, sadly, a consequent decline in the quality of work and a simplification and deterioration of traditional patterns.

Throughout the world the production of decorated textiles at home has died, mainly because industrialised manufacture has made an infinite range of textiles available at a fraction of the cost of a hand-made embroidery. This, together with the reluctance to spend the time necessary to weave and embroider, and the pressures of a conformist fashion culture, has brought about the end of the domestic art of embroidery.

4 The Cyclades

The Cyclades in the Western Aegean are composed of about twenty major islands and over a hundred smaller ones. In classical times they were seen as a single unit and later, together with Astypalaia, formed the Duchy of Naxos during the Frankish Empire. Even under the Ottomans they were treated as a single unit, administered by a Kapudan Pasha based in Naxos, with local Beys or Voivodes in the main islands. They were an original part of the New Greek Kingdom created in 1832, newly liberated from Ottoman rule.

I have chosen to study this group in three geographic areas, within which there is a certain similarity in the embroideries.

> *south-western*:   Pholegandros, Melos and Kimolos
> *south-eastern*:   Amorgos, Anafi, Ios, Sikinos and Astypalaia
> *central*:   Naxos, Paros and Siphnos
> *Italianate embroideries*

There is no distinguishably different embroidery tradition for the islands lying north of Naxos. Both Andros and Kythnos had Albanian populations that were moved there from Euboea in the early fifteenth century, after a period of depopulation. Further waves of Albanians arrived after the Turkish conquest at the beginning of the eighteenth century, so that by 1900 their descendants formed at least a third of the population of both islands. Even so I can trace no evidence of an Albanian style that would have been brought with the new populations in any of the Aegean embroideries, although Albanian and Slav influences are very evident in the embroideries of mainland Attica and Boeotia. The embroideries of the northern Cyclades and throughout the islands of the Saronic Gulf are so much part of the modern Greek style that it is impossible to trace the survival of any distinctive local styles, as one can in the other islands of the group.

Elsewhere the constant change in the levels of population in the islands must have affected the growth of a local style and tradition. It is probable that each new influx of population brought with it new and

A bolster from Naxos decorated with a green trellis filled with a quartered pattern. Both the trellis and the diamonds are filled with geometric Mamluk patterns. Formerly in the Mrs F H Cook collection (Plate 47 in *Mediterranean and Near East Embroideries*). Before 1700.

foreign styles, which were absorbed and added to a native tradition if they did not merely replace it. A Venetian report of 1563 states that only five of the sixteen islands belonging to the Dukes of Naxos were inhabited, and that of those five only one, Melos, was in a flourishing state. If this was true of the protected Duchy, how much more unstable the other islands of the Aegean must have been.

If all but very few of the embroideries date from after 1700, as I am sure must be the case, then they were made after the final conquest of the area by the Ottoman Turks, when the islands returned to a certain degree of calmness and stability, and were once more populated and engaged in commerce. They supplied both the large Turkish market and the accessible portion of the European market with cereals, raw materials, textiles, stockings and even mill stones. After the War of Independence there was yet another period of growth for the islands, based on the revival of a trading, commercial tradition and on the introduction of new industries. New commercial towns were created, such as Hermoupolis in Syra, which absorbed large numbers of Greeks fleeing from the Turks, and by 1834 it was the largest and most important port in the new Greece. This change in the fortune of the Aegean meant that a new middle class was created, based on the redistribution of the lands that had belonged to the now ousted and deteriorated Latin aristocracy. This change in the Aegean was a fore-

A scarf with one end laid over the other. The broad border has two upright plants set one above the other with blue birds set between them. The sides have a complicated plant form alternating with a large green bird. This simple bolia was converted into a small head covering. Siphnos or Kythnos, before 1800.

runner of the changes that were soon to take place on the mainland.

The main group of textiles in the Cyclades and also - as will be seen later - in the Dodecanese are those used to decorate the bed or the bed alcove. The forms that these bed furnishings take depends, quite naturally, on the position that the bed has in the interior architecture of the house. It is necessary to consider that fact before discussing the textiles themselves.

The use of embroidery for clothing in the Cyclades may have been more widespread than the surviving number of garments with embroidery would suggest. The main feature of Cycladic costume, according to Thévenot in 1664, was the number of skirts that were worn, one on top of another: 'so many that they impeded the women walking.' About seventy years later Tournefort, in his *Relation d'un Voyage au Levant*, mentions the heavy clothing worn, remarking how unattractive it was. He only mentions Mykonos as having embroidered costumes. If he was reporting correctly, then that tradition died very soon afterwards and the pieces have all disappeared, as none of the existing prints of the Mykonos costume of the period show any large-scale embroidery at all. The one piece of domestic embroidery, white silk on white, attributed to Mykonos, could have come from any island in the Aegean influenced by Venice.

I shall not refer to costume embroidery in the Cyclades, but will restrict myself to the large corpus of domestic embroidery made for

The corner of a sheet worked in blocks of two geometric patterns. The simple design and work are typical of Kythnos. About 1800.

household use. Equally, I shall not attempt to discuss the many pieces of white drawn thread work; they follow a different, more universal style and tradition, and although they do draw on the standard repertoire of motifs, they are not so different from each other, and it is futile to attempt to attribute them to any specific island.

The traditional house in the Cyclades during the fifteenth to seventeenth centuries is a single-room building, described as *kamares* in the documents. This house was usually part of an irregular terrace fronting onto a street, sometimes with a short flight of steps. The terrace might either be on a level or follow the irregular lie of the terrain. Inside the house the single room was divided by a vault in the shape of an arch, locally called *volto*. The front portion was the main living area and the rear contained the kitchen, store room and sleeping chambers. The back was sometimes divided into two levels, with the bed set in a built wooden alcove above the storage space. In grander plans, the bed is set on a mezzanine floor above both a kitchen and storage area. The bed in the raised alcove is reached by a short, small box, *pankos*, set on a longer box, *parapankos* or *sofas*, forming a simple set of steps. The bed on the raised mezzanine, which is also called *sofas* or *krevata*, is reached by a flight of stairs, which may themselves contain a storage cupboard. p.89

The bed in the alcove or on the sofas is the main bed and usually double, supplemented by a single bed in the front room, used as a seat during the day, or by a small bed on casters which can be stored under a bench or even under the main bed. This is called the *krevatsoula* in the Greek houses and *cariola*, after the Italian *cariruola*, in the Latin houses.

The main bed was always curtained off, and it is these curtains, with their accompanying bolsters and cushions, that form the great treasure of Cycladic embroidery. The bed furnishings are elaborate and were designed to make the bed the focal and most important feature in the house. The set consists of curtains in front of the bed, with or without a defined door, occasionally with curtains set against the wall behind the bed. Where there is no top decorative border worked onto the curtain panels, there may even be a separate pelmet hung from the ceiling; this is usually found on a bed set on the mezzanine balcony. Finally, a number of cushions are piled in a stack outside the curtains on the topmost box step, with the embroidered edges on one or two sides showing as a pillar.

In many of the houses of the north Cyclades, as in the Sporades, the bed was not a permanent built-in feature of the house; it was made up on the floor of either the main room or of the raised balcony. The bedding was stored during the day in wall cupboards, called *musandres*, from the Turkish *musandira*. In these cases there are no embroidered curtains; at most there is an embroidered quilt cover or a woven counterpane, or even an embroidered sheet, and the inevitable cushions. Perhaps it is this lack of a permanent bed that most inhibited the development of a local embroidery style in many of the islands.

The usual set of Cycladic bed curtains is made of strips of domestic

p.39

woven linen, 47–53 cm wide and a maximum of 330 cm long, embroidered with coloured silk in satin and darning stitch. The front curtains are composed of two separate leaves, each of three or four panels, sewn selvedge to selvedge with a fishbone stitch, *psarokokkalo* or with an insert of a narrow woven ribbon. The bed is entered through an informal door, which is merely a gap between the two leaves of the curtains. The back curtain – when it exists, and it is quite rare – is composed of five to seven strips, also sewn selvedge to selvedge to make one large panel, usually much more lightly decorated than the front curtains. This usage of bed curtains does not require the panels to be tapered from top to bottom: they remain the same width and hang straight down from either a rod or a batten fixed to the ceiling.

Each panel width of the curtain is embroidered with a design that is completely contained within it, allowing one to assume that each panel was worked separately before being joined to the next. This also accounts for the slight misalignments of the design and the changes in colours found between panels. It is only on Naxos that the strips are joined and then over-embroidered with an all-over pattern worked over the seams.

The decoration on the curtains is invariably composed of a rising column of a repeat pattern, with a broad band of the same pattern at the bottom or, more rarely, at the top. In Naxos and Siphnos a different pattern is used which will be described later. Back curtains, if decorated at all, have one slight vertical strip of a small pattern running up the centre of each panel.

Pholegandros, Melos and Kimolos

The oldest pieces of embroidery have all been attributed to this group of islands, particularly to Pholegandros, with one particular pattern attributed to Melos. Melos is the larger island and has had a continuous settled population for the longest time. It was the most important centre in the Cyclades after Andros and Naxos. Thévenot estimates the population at about 3000 in 1655, growing to about 6000–7000 by 1730, with the majority of the inhabitants living in the main city. After the Ottoman occupation of 1579 it was the centre of the French trading activity in the Aegean, and became an important entrepôt for trade.

It is at about the time of Melos' greatest importance that these curtains were probably made, and it is likely that they were made in Melos rather than Pholegandros, although it is not possible to be absolutely sure. However, Pholegandros was always an unimportant island, with no natural resources and a small population that was introduced into an island that was deserted in medieval times. In 1715 the island was attacked by the Turkish Admiral Canim Hoca, who deported the whole population. There can not have been very much embroidery carried out there at that time. Melos itself was devastated by 1770, which may account for the lack of any curtains of a second period. There are only about eight complete sets of the old version of these curtains left, so they were not all that common even when they were being made, in about 1675-1750. If they were professional rather than domestic work, as I believe, then they represented a very considerable expenditure for the families, and would been even more valuable than jewellery.

The pattern in the oldest examples is an elaborate development of patterns that bear very considerable similarities to Mamluk embroideries of the fourteenth century. These similarities have been noted before, and they occur again outside this group, particularly in the curtains generally attributed to Patmos. There are two basic but p.67 similar varieties of the design, varying only in detail from one set to another. The decoration covers 80-85 per cent of the total surface of each panel, and is based on a broad central column which covers just over half the width of the panel, with the same design used as a border at the base of each panel, forming an integral valance. In this position the pattern is scaled up and lightly bulked out to be equal to three-quarters of the width of the panel. On both edges of each panel there is a slighter column of another pattern.

The central main column in the first type is composed of units of two chevrons set vertically opposite each other, with a string of five small diamonds stretched between their inner angles, making the spine of the column. Each pair of chevrons is joined to the next by a diamond containing four small swastikas. Between the facing ends of the chevrons there are a pair of the same diamonds, but in this position they contain only one swastika. From the outside of each of these diamonds there springs a multibranched tree terminating in a very simplified bird, which is itself flanked by a pair of opposed crested and starry-tailed stylized birds. The diamond containing four small swastikas in each quarter is flanked on each side by a complicated figure composed of a pair of opposed dogs, joined at the tail so as to make a two-headed animal, with the front feet converted into wings. This figure becomes a two-headed dog-eagle. Between the two heads there is another swastika diamond, from which a further multi-branch tree rises.

The whole pattern is extremely light, even if it is filled out with a variety of small branched shapes, diamonds and pairs of very skinny erect lions, with every line of the chevron and multi-branched trees festooned with latch hooks. This lightness can partly be attributed to the fact that although the main column is in red, the birds and dog figures are worked in a soft gold and a green-blue, which emphasise the transparency of the whole design.

The pattern of the two subsidiary outside columns is a simple chevron, rather like a sycamore seed, containing a basic diamond filled with a cross, flanked by two diamonds containing the angular dog, and finally a chequered triangle to complete the chevron. This whole pattern is densely collapsed onto itself.

The second type, of which two forms exist, has a much narrower

Cushions from the Dodecanese. These cushions were part of the standard house furnishing, usually stacked in columns by the bed, with the decorated sides showing. *Top left to bottom right* Kos, Chios, Tilos, Nisyros, Nisyros, Chios.

central column which is not based on the vertical spine of facings chevrons. In one, the column is based on a pole running through two alternating shapes, a diamond filled with four swastikas and a latched 'S', surrounded with an eight-petalled star. The sycamore-seed outer columns are simplified and strung on a small leafed figure. The other is again the simplified pole version, but the two shapes are flanked by square versions of the eight-petalled star. Both have the sycamore-seed outer columns.

In another, possibly later, version the solid column is replaced by series of a simplified *spitha* set in alternating colours in isolation, one above the other. This spitha has a very simple chevron with three candelabra shapes rising up from it, the centre one taller than the other two, with a pair of opposed birds set about its column. It also appears in the bottom border.

p.146

In the Benaki Museum, one panel, attributed to Patmos by Wace, is like the first design but the two opposite halves of the pattern have been slipped half a drop, so that the chevron pattern has become a strong serpentine ribbon band filled with swastikas, or with fylfots and a large 'S' pattern, and the double-bodied dog now has a fylfot in a diamond set between its two heads, giving the curtain a quite different appearance, although clearly belonging to the same tradition.

Ten curtain strips attributed to Melos all come from a single set of curtains purchased by Wace and now distributed between four museums. In this set the central column is composed of the Mamluk branch set vertically about a spine of rhomboids filled with a diagonal design, separated by a small diamond filled with the swastika that Wace calls a millsail. The central spine is here edged with a broken twisted ribbon on both sides. The outer edges of each panel have an ascending Mamluk branch pattern, inset with opposed dogs. They are worked in a pale monochrome red silk in satin and darning stitch, and where it remains, they all have the identical red and white silk stitch joining the panels.

The embroidery on all the pieces is carried out in polychrome untwisted silk with red predominating, being at least 80 per cent of all the colour used, with touches of violet, gold, and a lustrous white.

Some strips attributed to Pholegandros bear a similarity to these curtains, but they are clearly later creations, possibly mid to late nineteenth century. They draw on the earlier style; their simplification and adaptation is unsympathetic, and although the embroidery is still worked very finely in polychrome silks on a domestic linen, it is now worked in cross stitch, long-armed cross stitch and chain stitch, in addition to the satin and darning stitches. In one, the Mamluk branch and peacock design is set about a column of rhomboids filled with an Italianate tracery, and edged with a foreign carnation border, and two new colours have been added to the earlier ones: altogether an ugly and debased development. Another, in Boston, is equally awkward and corrupt. In it the central column of the Mamluk branch is flanked by isolated motifs of animals and plant patterns within an outer border of a more conventional filled geometric pattern of a running wave and a small two-leaf flower. The isolation of the motives and the lack of cohesion of the embroidery suggests a later use of the various elements without any understanding of the initial inspiration.

The curtains in this group are generally about 195 cm long, and each panel is 45 cm wide, made of a very fine linen which must be a home-woven product rather than a bought fabric. The silk used is a fine lightly twisted yarn and again gives the impression of being a domestically spun thread dyed red at home.

Pieces at the V&A Museum and the Ashmolean Museum attributed to Kimolos all bear a design very different to anything else in the Cyclades. They were originally labelled by Myres as Kalymnos, which seems more likely, having been made during the Ottoman occupation of the Dodecanese, and these will be discussed in that section.

Four panels forming one of a pair of curtains for a bed in an alcove. Each has a central column of a six-sided Mamluk cartouche with a twisted ribbon running the length of the panel. A large spitha set with birds and a smaller spitha are placed sideways. The borders on each panel are formed of small spithas set closely above each other. The other curtain is in the Victoria & Albert Museum (T.763-1877). Melos, about 1750.

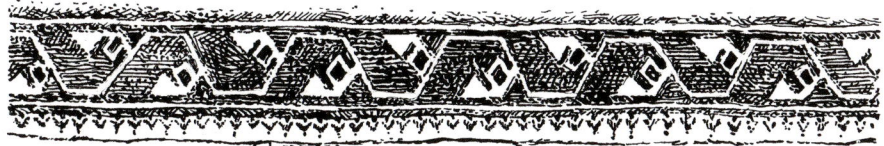

Amorgos, Anafi, Ios, Sikinos and Astypalaia

This group includes the embroideries attributed to Amorgos and Anafi, that produced a large volume of textiles, and to Ios and Sikinos, that produced much less. It also includes those embroideries made in Astypalaia that are part of the Cycladic tradition.

The embroideries from this group differ from those of the south-western group in two main respects. One is the use of pattern, which in Amorgos amounts to an almost monomaniacal dedication to one main pattern and to one border or edging pattern. The other is the basic shape of the pieces embroidered, and this is accounted for by how the bed was placed and used. The majority of the embroideries was made for decorating the bed, and in these islands the beds were placed on a raised balcony, the sofa, rather than in an alcove. They are consequently much shorter, being only 140 cm long, and are made of a coarse hand-woven linen in strips 40 cm wide.

The bed curtains are composed of two leaves, each of four widths, without different door panels. The panels are usually sewn selvedge to selvedge, or joined with a red and white fishbone stitch. The quality of these embroideries varies from very fine to rather coarse, as does the quality of the linen.

The textiles from Amorgos are almost exclusively decorated with the broad-leaf pattern, which Wace calls the 'king pattern', but which is called in Greek *bradyfyllo*, *spathofyllo* or *platyfyllo*. The pattern is composed of two identical leaves set at an angle to each other and joined at the stalk. In Amorgos the pattern is set in long vertical columns with the pairs of leaves either telescoped onto each other or springing from a central feathered spine. The design is always contained within each panel and can be set out in two, three or four identical columns. The bottom border is a horizontal band of two or three pairs of the leaves, or of some detail of the pattern set out to fill the space between the columns. A narrow border of a double axe and triangle is used almost exclusively in Amorgos. The only stitch used is long or short darning stitch.

p.148

The placing of the bed meant that no horizontal valance was necessary, and those pieces described as valances are more likely to be shelf cloths. They are found edged with a heavy fringe on a dagged edge, which is unusual for a bed valance but which would have great effect on a shelf used either for displaying the family icons, plates and pottery, or even on a fireplace mantelshelf.

Other than bed curtains, the main embroidered textiles found are cushions, usually embroidered in darning stitch in the Amorgos colours, and are either single or double faced. The commonest pattern is again the double leaf, but more general geometric patterns are also found which are very reminiscent of the work from Anafi, a neighbouring island.

The colour range used here is much softer than in the south-western group; the green is gentler, the reds are more varied, and a gold-brown

is introduced. The embroideries are in either a monochrome red, or a sequence of red, green, red and gold-brown, giving the appearance of a red embroidery relieved with other colours. The red used in Amorgos is reputed to have been made from a lichen which grew on rocks at the sea edge. The lichen is either *Rocella tinctoria*, which is the source of the colouring chemical called *orchil*, or it is *Variolaria orcina*, from which *orcin* is derived. Whichever it may have been, it was known in the islands as oricello, and produced the very particular red and violet found in amorgine work. The only stitch used is darning stitch, sometimes worked as a stem or tent stitch.

p.44

The embroideries from Anafi are all made with cross and long-armed cross stitch, and occasionally a brick stitch, rather than the darning stitch of Amorgos.

The majority of the embroideries attributed to Anafi are rectangular cushion covers and pieces that are called valances. They were mainly collected by Wace when he was in Anafi in about 1906, and then augmented by others bought in Athens. He states that he thought that he was one of the first to collect in Anafi, and at that time there must still have been a considerable volume of embroideries in the island. He sees in the work on the Anafi cushions patterns that have survived from pre-classical Greece and then developed in classical Greece; a pleasant if unsupportable proposition. The patterns are all developments of geometric shapes, and in that sense are similar to designs used in antiquity, but it is not tenable to see them as uninterrupted survivals. They are not exclusive to Anafi; one sees the same patterns in Amorgos cushions and further afield in Kos and Chios, and even in Thasos in the north.

A cloth used for the shelf on which icons were displayed. Plant forms in red alternating with blue and green are set between narrow borders of stylized flowers, with an outer pattern unusually cut into dags with tassels. Found in Amorgos. Before 1800.

The two main collections of Anafi are at the V&A Museum and at Liverpool. The V&A collection of about twenty pieces comes from Dawkins, and that at Liverpool of thirty-six pieces, of which twenty are cushions, were part of the Wace purchase. There are many pairs of cushions worked with the same pattern, and we must assume that this was common practice.

Some pieces from Anafi have been identified as valances; they all have the same basic shape, embroidered on the long and two short edges of a single panel of linen, usually 190 cm long and the usual 40-50 cm deep. This shape makes one doubt that they were conventional valances: it is hard to see how they would have been used. The fact that no bed curtains have survived from Anafi, Ios or Sikinos would support the theory that these pieces were not used with a curtained bed but with a free-standing one, or with the put-away bed, in which case they may have been the embroidered ends of counterpanes or sheets. They are very similar to surviving sheets where the decoration is applied in lace or drawn thread work around three sides of the panel. It is not possible to define their exact usage and perhaps it would be wrong to insist on only one usage, but to consider them as decorative panels used wherever and whenever needed.

These panels are not decorated in the same style or patterns as the cushions, although they use the same range of cross and long-armed cross stitches. The V&A has two embroidered panels, which had been collected by Dawkins and which he says were used together as a double valance. The top one has the outer ends turned inwards, the embroidery having been done on the wrong side to allow for this, and then the folded sheet is set on top of, and within, the embroidered border of the lower sheet. There are three pairs of these sheets in Liverpool, one of which has been cut and resewn so that the decoration is all on one side.

The Benaki has a small collection of drawn thread and filled work attributed to Anafi. I think that these are all the ends of small towels re-cycled into a long strip that does now look like the border of a bedspread. The patterns are all those found on the bed sheets or spreads of this area, although they do have a look of the Ionian Islands about them.

The other islands in this group are Ios, or Nios, as it is also called, and Sikinos. They are both very small and have always had small populations: by 1828 they did not total 2000 inhabitants together. It is therefore not surprising that there are few surviving embroideries from them, and most of these were collected by Wace and Dawkins during their visits there about 1906.

The surviving pieces are mainly sheet borders, bed spreads or cushions. They are similar to those of Anafi in that they are worked in the range of cross stitches on linen or cotton, and are not part of the usual form of Cycladic bed furnishings. The lengths that are to be seen in various museums are always identified as valances, but they are more likely to be the surviving embroidered ends of sheets, as in Anafi. The

patterns used are more varied than those found in Anafi. They are not exclusively geometric but are small blocks of repeated patterns which include simplified lions and multi-legged animals and the fat-tailed birds that one sees in the Ionian embroideries. These animal designs are alternated with representations of vases and various floral motifs.

p.44

There are very few pieces attributed specifically to Sikinos, and most of them are narrow bands of embroidery that may have been the edging of either sheets or rather flimsy curtains. They are all worked in brick stitch or a small stem stitch on a very fine linen gauze, which is more like the *mulham*, described in the next section under Siphnos, than the robust linen of the other islands. The patterns are those general to the area, but because they are worked in brick stitch they are given a bulk and solidity that is unique.

p.156

Two pieces in the Fitzwilliam Museum were bought in Sikinos, the first composed of three panels and which could be one leaf of a pair of bed curtains. This piece has no borders at either end and can only be seen as directional from the fat birds that are scattered all over it. The lower ends of two of the panels have been later worked by a different, less expert, hand. It is important because one would expect there to be bed curtains in the island, and no others have survived. The other piece is a long strip, embroidered with a border at both ends of the typical elongated motifs in stem stitch and a narrow border down one edge. This piece may come from a garment. The fabric is very light, as is the whole impression of the work.

Astypalaia lies equidistant from Amorgos and Anafi in the Cyclades and from Kos in the Dodecanese It was part of the Cycladic Duchy of Naxos but is today part of the Dodecanese. The embroideries made there belong to both traditions and present considerable problems in classification. I have placed the island in two different groups, first here within the south-eastern Cycladic group, so as to discuss those pieces that include designs similar to those of Anafi and Ios. However, the bulk

One end of a hand towel worked on linen in darning stitch to look like weaving. The other end is in the Victoria & Albert Museum (T.636-1950). Both pieces have been cut to make something else and then rejoined. Collected together by Dawkins and Wace in 1910 and shared betwen them. Cycladic, Crete(?) before 1850.

43

of Astypalaian work is part of a Dodecanese tradition and will be discussed later in that chapter.

As part of the Duchy it was more easily approached from the Cyclades than from Rhodes, and must have been influenced at an earlier time by fashion from the Cyclades and then later by its connection with Rhodes. The island was repopulated by the Sanudo family in 1413 with part of the population from Tinos, which might explain the Cycladic form of Astypalaian embroidery but, more interestingly, might also indicate that even by the beginning of the fifteenth century there was a style that was distinctly Cycladic that could be transferred to the Dodecanese.

Astypalaia remained an island that kept to ancient traditions which it had maintained from the time when it was within the Byzantine Empire, and partly under control of the Byzantine Monastery of Our Lady of Khozoviotissa in Amorgos. Its especial character was preserved by its isolation and the ambiguity of its allegiance. The women's costume of the island remained more like that of Byzantium longer even than Hellenistic Epirus, and survived until the Italian occupation in the 1920s.

The corner of a sheet worked unusually in gold-coloured silk in block stitch. The end shows a fig tree with birds, the side has a composite mythical beast with a long neck and an extravagant set of horns. The embroidery in red, brown and green appears to have been added later by a different hand. Siphnos or Kythnos, before 1800.

The Astypalaian pieces that are Cycladic in style are pieces of costume, mainly skirts, that carry borders of birds, animals, ships and vases. They are worked on either linen or cotton. The accepted view is that the older pieces are linen and the more recent cotton, but this should only be accepted as a very broad definition. The patterns are all contained units, and are fairly simple in construction. They bear some resemblance to designs found in Skyros, Epirus and even Crete but they are not copies of them; they are more likely to be derived from the same Italian originals. The skirt borders are exceptional in that they again demonstrate the wide range of influences on the island. The motifs are similar to those from the eastern Cyclades, particularly the bed sheets from Anafi and Ios, with which they share the sailing vessel, the small sailors, the horsemen and the small fat bird known as the Anafi partridge.

p.43

Additionally, they use the dixos from the central islands of the Dodecanese, but unlike all the other embroideries from the area they also portray strange animals such as camels which are often ridden by little men, elaborately tailed long-necked horses, stylised birds with their tails in display, called *perdikes zervodexies,* and a very stylised form of the Byzantine double-headed eagle. They also portray two types of vessels, the *karavi* and the *dilinia*, ships of the line, all manned by little manikins.

The embroiderers of Astypalaia also over-embroidered existing pieces with their own native designs. There are a number of these pieces, the majority of which are standard Turkish *çevre* already embroidered at the ends or on all four sides, which have been converted to church use by having little churches or church buildings embroidered on them. These are known as baptismal cloths and were used to wrap the child's head when it was being annointed with holy water. There is one such cloth in the Cincinnati Art Museum where the ground is filled with the whole repertoire of Astypalaian design.

A bed sheet worked on two faces so that when one is folded over on the bed both right sides will be seen. The pattern is a deteriorated version of a coat of arms, possibly Crispi, showing heraldic birds and tulips. Anafi, about 1750.

A wider range of stitches is used in Astypalaia than in any of the other islands. In addition to the expected cross stitch they also use a small back stitch and a buttonhole edging stitch. The range of colours of the twisted silks is larger than other islands of this group, including slate blue, mauve and pink in the later pieces. Most units of the patterns are worked in one colour, with alternating patterns in different colours.

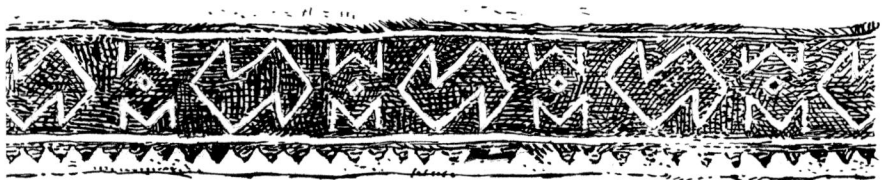

Naxos, Paros and Siphnos

The embroideries of Naxos are the masterpieces of Cycladic embroidery. They are instantly recognisable and can also be attributed with confidence to Naxos: there is a long series of evidence, from travellers to the island, mainly Jesuits visiting their parishioners in what was the largest Catholic community in the islands, and others from the earliest pilgrims in the eleventh century, right up to Theodore Bent writing at the end of the nineteenth century. He refers to visiting the Latin families of Naxos who lived on the hill, and seeing 'their treasures of embroidery and jewellery preserved since the Venetian days.' Finally, the very comprehensive island dowry and marriage documents and series of wills refer to Naxian red-embroidered long cushion covers from the beginning of the seventeenth century right up to the 1840s.

Naxos was the seat of the Duchy of Naxos and the capital of the Cyclades from 1210 until the Ottoman occupation of 1579. It was the centre of the Catholic Latin church in the island; the combined diocese of Paros and Naxos, Paronaxia, was the most important of the seven dioceses of the Byzantine Church in the Cyclades. After the formation of the duchy a Roman Bishop was appointed in about 1320, and he controlled a cathedral on each island. The Roman Church existed side by side with the remaining structure of the Byzantine Orthodox Church, which retained its cathedral, the Ekatonpylai in Paros. Even during the Ottoman occupation Naxos preserved separate Latin and Greek churches and societies.

All the islands in the Cyclades were directly connected to Italy through the Italian lords of the islands, the Crispi and Barozzi of Naxos, the Condestaulo of Andros and Siphnos, the Ghisi of Mykonos and Tinos and the Querini of Astypalaia. Through these families they were linked directly to Venice and influenced by the fashion there. The islands possessed the wealth to allow them to indulge in imported products, and the new nobility made a point of preserving their connections with Italy. The embroideries, therefore, are different to other Cycladic work, with a distinct European look based on patterns that were circulating in cultivated Italian society and derived from the new pattern books for embroidery and lace-making that were being printed in Venice. The embroideries were, most probably, originally done exclusively by the Latin community, the women, like their counterparts in rich society in Europe, devoting themselves to religion and domestic handicrafts. This style certainly prevailed throughout society in the Cyclades, and influenced embroidery as far afield as the northern islands of Thasos and Samothrace and the nearer island of Skyros.

As in all the other islands of the Aegean, the main embroidered pieces are those associated with the bed. Bed curtains from Naxos and Siphnos differ from other Cycladic bed furnishings in one main respect: the decoration on the curtains and cushions is invariably of an over-all pattern, embroidered after the panels of the ground linen have been sewn together selvedge to selvedge, therefore running over the sewn edges of the panels. The materials are the usual Cycladic ones; the basic fabric is linen, 17 x 20 threads per square centimetre, usually hand woven in panels 42-50 cm wide. The embroidery is carried out in untwisted floss silk that would have been spun and dyed locally. In Naxos a darning stitch is always used while in Siphnos it is satin stitch; in a practical sense the patterns used dictate the most appropriate stitch.

The embroideries from Naxos demonstrate how a basic theme and pattern was developed and elaborated over a long period. The main pattern is usually a repeated elongated diamond shape, like a geometric leaf, set within a diagonal trellis. The diamond shape and the counterpoint of stars and other versions of the diamond form large circular shapes with many flat sides. The variety of the basic diamond is vast, and the beauty of these fabrics is derived from the way in which the complexity of the basic forms allows the pattern to be read in many ways. This is accentuated by the fact that the untwisted floss silk is laid in two directions, so that light is reflected to make it appear that the monochrome red of the embroidery is two different tones of red. The monochrome red is sometimes highlighted by intrusions of blue, green and, more rarely, a brown-gold.

The origin of the basic geometric leaf pattern, set in rhomboids forming large circular shapes, can be traced to Mamluk decorative designs seen in their tiles, woodwork, cut plaster and textiles. The patterns are also similar to lace patterns from the handbooks published in Europe from the middle of the sixteenth century, which themselves may have been inspired by Mamluk originals. A trade connection between Venice and Mamluk Egypt had existed since the tenth century.

These patterns are used in two ways. The first, and most common, accounting for 90 per cent of all the surviving examples, is a dense over-all pattern covering the ground fabric totally, leaving unworked outlines in white. The second takes small details of the main patterns and sets them in parallel rows all over the ground fabric, leaving large

p.149

Overleaf Details of panels of Naxian bed curtains worked in stem stitch in floss silk. Eighteenth and nineteenth centuries. *Page 48* The stitches are laid in two directions, leaving the white base cloth to form the patterns, which are derived from Islamic geometric work not dissimilar to Fez work. *Page 49* Here much larger areas of the white backcloth are left, giving the impression of a woven cloth.

areas of the white background visible. The small design units are sometimes set in a half drop to vary the density of the textile. These Naxian patterns have their nearest equivalents in the monochrome embroideries from Fez, which are even today still offered as Greek pieces. These pieces are not copies of Greek work but rather share the common source and inspiration of Mamluk Egypt and Italy, a connection which existed many centuries before the Ottomans conquered and started to influence Islamic north African art.

Relatively few complete sets of bed curtains have survived. They have deteriorated either because the weight of embroidery has torn the linen or because the use of the bed hangings changed with fashion and the curtains were converted into bolsters, cushions or small covers, or wall hangings. It is an accepted part of the mythography propounded to account for the large number of fragments offered for sale that they are the result of the dividing up of old embroidery to ensure that each descendant received a portion of the parents' wealth. I have yet to be convinced by this story. The wills that have been studied never mention that any embroidery is to be cut up and divided between the inheritors.

The curtains were composed of two separate leaves, each about 166-200 cm long by 115-45 cm wide, made up of 3, 3½ or 4 widths, sewn selvedge to selvedge. They were made to measure to be hung in bed niches of different sizes without a valance. The embroidery is worked in running darning stitch worked over three threads, in a continuous repeat pattern contained within a narrow outer border, 6 cm wide, consisting of a simple running pattern within two lines. There would be no differently embroidered panel to indicate the entrance or to act as a door opening. The set of furnishings would have included cushions and bolsters, for which very spectacular covers were made.

Apart from these bed furnishings Naxos also produced wall hangings to be used behind either the bench or spare bed in the main room, although I believe that this was a much later development. The bed curtains were of such a shape and size that they were easily adapted for hanging on the wall, and may have given rise to the production of these hangings once the use of the bed in the house was changed to a later European style. These are double the size of the long bolsters, two lengths sewn together, usually with a red silk fishbone stitch, to form a square. They have been described as table cloths, but there are no obvious uses for table covers of this size as there were very few occasional tables in existence at that time; nor are they double-faced bolster covers. They must be the wall hangings to decorate the area above the bench or spare bed in the front room.

The bolsters have generally remained uncut and they, more than any other pieces, show the genius of Naxos embroidery: an ability to invent variations on a standard theme, using this invention not only for the basic diamond pattern and containing trellis but also for the narrow guard border used on all the pieces. The invention is even carried into the use of colour, and the occasional introduction of other colours,

p.30

The edge of a head cloth on cotton gauze decorated with gold birds set about a large plant reminiscent of a simple spitha. Siphnos, about 1750.

p.137, 181

highlighting the exclusive monochrome red with a soft green and a clear blue, sometimes placed in the centre of the main pattern, or to form the elaborate trellis, or even in the outer guard border.

The rectangular bolsters are always single-faced, unlike the square cushions of the other islands which have embroidery on three edges of both faces. The bolsters are embroidered in the same technique as the curtains, often in pairs with designs to match the curtains. The bolsters are 110-35 cm long and 40-50 cm wide, again with the repeat pattern contained within a narrow ribbon border. There are a number of standard versions of this border: I have seen about forty different ones which are variations on about ten basic themes. Although these are all basically Naxian designs, they are found throughout Greece, even in mainland embroideries. I think that they have all been developed by the island embroiderers and are not necessarily direct copies of any extant patterns.

Because of the shape and use of the bed in Naxos there are no examples of valances or bed tents to be found that can be definitely attributed to this central group of the Cyclades, and although the group displays the widest development of a theme in terms of pattern, the usage of the textiles is confined to the bed curtains, bolsters and wall hangings.

There are very few pieces that can be unarguably attributed specifically to Paros. One would expect Paros work to be very similar to Naxos: they are too close to have developed distinctly different work, although that cannot be a rule. Wace developed a theory that the embroidery was very similar to Skyran work on the basis that Paros had been repopulated at some time with peoples from the Northern Cyclades and the Sporades, and that in certain villages a dialect was spoken that was similar to that of the north. He attributed to Paros a very famous piece of embroidery that he had collected which portrayed horsemen; this raised a great storm in Greek circles and his

A small cushion with a pattern of small dogs and a simple flower on one side and deer alternating with a larger plant. This naively worked piece was collected by Wace in 1906 from Paros. He comments that it is the only piece he ever found on the island. Paros, about 1800.

attribution was strongly criticised; it is now universally accepted that the piece is almost certainly from Epirus and will be discussed in that section. Having decided that this piece was from Paros, he then attributed to Paros a number of pieces that were similar, and they were identified as such in the Liverpool exhibition of 1956. All these are now accepted as standard Sporadic work.

There is one piece that Wace did collect in Paros, a small cushion to which he attached a note saying, 'Paros, bought there.' The rectangular cushion is embroidered on three edges of both faces in a very Naxian red. The design has a band of a geometric pattern surmounted by a panel of alternating horselike animals and a small branch. This is quite close to the work done in the neighbouring southern island of Ios.

p.51

Very few embroideries are today attributed to Siphnos and they clearly all belong to the same tradition, if not to the same sets of hangings. The main examples that have survived of this tradition are strips from pieces that may have been curtains, but sadly no complete set ofcurtains has survived which would prove that assumption. The pieces are all worked on a very fine loose textured linen or cotton very similar to *mulham*, a union of cotton and silk. Lord Charlemont, in his travels in the islands in 1749, mentions that the islands of Tinos and Kythnos: 'having an abundance of the best silk and of cotton, which they make into a sort of yellow gauze, extremely pretty, and used by the women for veils,' showing that even in the middle of the eighteenth century the islands were still producing woven material that would have been available in neighbouring islands for embroidery. It is not true that at that time the manufacture of cotton stockings, which were imported into France in great quantities, was the only activity of the islands.

The embroidery from Siphnos is all in a very lustrous silk in satin stitch. The pattern is the typical one of vertical columns of a simplified branch pattern, very similar to the *spitha* of Kos work. In Siphnos the arms of the branch are festooned with latch hooks, making the whole look like the branches of a monkey puzzle tree. These upright columns are sometimes interspersed with rows of little figures of men in baggy trousers and women in skirts, each with one hand on a hip and the other raised to the head, alternating with rows of long-legged pairs of angular birds.

p.152

The other type of embroidery attributed to Siphnos, but much less securely so, consists of two narrow strips, 270 cm long and only 10 cm wide, again with silk embroidery in satin stitch on linen in gold, brown and a little blue in the edging. They are clearly from the textile which was collected by Dawkins and Wace together. I think they are the edgings of a large cloth and possibly not a curtain at all. The work is similar to Melos work from the south-western Cyclades, and might belong to that group.

A curtain of four panels is clearly from the same group but is quite different from that described above, with a unique placing of the decoration, concentrated on the top border, substituting as a pelmet.

The pattern is a standard Mamluk branch set above a pair of broad leaves, themselves placed above a pair of rhomboids filled with a horizontal 'S'. The vertical column on each panel is formed of opposed broad leaves in pairs, alternately large and small, which are not set in the middle of the panel but on one or both outer edges. This set of curtains must have been made for a particular location, most probably a bed set on a raised sofa behind a balustrade, where the top of the curtain would be more visible than the bottom. It may be a fusion of the Pholegandros and Amorgos types, mainly because of the introduction of the broad leaf pattern, but it also could be a fusion of basic Cycladic types.

p.179 The only other piece attributed to Siphnos is the bed curtain on the bed set up in the Burlington Fine Arts Club exhibition as exhibit no. 68. This is much more likely to be from Ios, Anafi or even Astypalaia. The work is carried out in a cross stitch rather than the darning and satin stitch of the group, and it is a top-bordered curtain much more like the curtains from those islands. The pattern of ships and men would also indicate Ios.

The corner of a small cloth decorated with large horned deer alternating with a large plant. Worked in an unsteady stem stitch in floss silk on cotton gauze. Ios, before 1800.

53

Italianate embroideries

The influence of Italy on the Cyclades has been referred to many times previously, mainly to show how specific fashions or motifs were derived from Italy. However, a group of embroideries found extensively in the Cyclades is more than the product of ideas derived from Italian work. These embroideries are strictly within the Italian tradition but are not copies. They were worked by the Latins and Franks living in the islands but following styles from home. Although they were made in the Cyclades and found there, they are not Greek island work in my understanding of the term. The same applies to the pieces of Italianate lace that are attributed to Melos.

They are mainly the sleeve ends and neck bands of shirts, but also borders of sheets or long narrow cloths, linen hand towels of every sort and the decorative edges of church trappings or clerical garments. They are invariably worked in monochrome silk on linen, in green or red, and are in Italian two-sided cross stitch or in long-armed cross stitch.

The patterns are the long friezes of wreath patterns or even the

Above An embroidered strip used as a table decoration. It is copied directly from one of the pattern books published in Venice from the middle of the sixteenth century and available in the islands. The piece is made up of imported linen strips cobbled together and over-embroidered in two-sided Italian cross stitch. Cycladic, probably Latin Naxos, about 1720.

Left A sheet end of a twisted vine set with sea monsters, winged horses, dragons and other mythical beasts, converted to a ribbon with added overcast edges and tassels. These strips were commonly used in churches, draped over icon and bible stands. Another portion of this strip is in the Victoria & Albert Museum (T.447D-1950). Naxos or Melos, before 1750.

Right An embroidered mach-ramas copying a woven towel from Perugia. The winged lion is the Venetian Marzoco, the two-headed eagle is the symbol of Byzantium. These cloths were often used as baptismal towels, afterwards donated to the church and used as humeral veils. Astypalaia, about 1750.

renaissance pattern of a frieze with grotesques. These were certainly used as table or chest covers in Latin households, or even as altar frontals. The wreath patterns are also often found as a sleeve trim on Astypalain shirts.

The other group of Italianate fabrics is that from Astypalaia, which to my mind is part of the Italian Cycladic influence; these are the towels in drawn thread work where both ends are decorated with a panel of winged griffons, birds, heraldic lions and double-headed eagles, resembling Perugia towels rather than anything in the Aegean. These towels or headscarves are a linen-silk fabric with a panel of plain linen at both ends. The embroidery is filled drawn-thread work in white on a blue ground, with details in a coral red, and again, unlike anything else in the Greek island tradition, these pieces are double-faced.

5 *The Dodecanese*

The thirteen islands of the Dodecanese lie along the Aegean coast of Turkey, forming a less homogenous unit than the Cyclades. As elsewhere in the Aegean, the Dodecanese developed a tradition of decoration which was a fusion of all the influences on the area and, as in the Cyclades, the main form of domestic decoration was embroidery.

The largest island, Rhodes, was the centre of the Knights Hospitaller and the commercial heart of the medieval traders with the East. The Knights formed a considerable community both in power and numbers; it is estimated that by 1514, just before the third and final siege of the island, the population had risen to over 550 knights, with an army of about 5000 mercenaries alongside a civilian population of another 5000. The Knights lived in great luxury, abandoning their original role as 'Servants to our Lord the Poor'. Their main activity was the legitimate one of acting as middlemen for the great pilgrim traffic of the Middle Ages, and as suppliers of eastern goods for the European market. They protected this legitimate trade by attacking, as mercenaries, the Ottoman fleet, but they also operated as opportunistic pirates, indiscriminately raiding for loot both Christian and non-Christian vessels in the Mediterranean. The knighthood was composed of the sons of noble families and they used their acquired wealth to make their lives more comfortable, mainly by introducing into the islands the habits and customs of patrician society in Europe, one of which would have been the gentility of the secluded bed.

The islands were important as fortified military posts but were also centres for the development of new industries, particularly textile and leather, based on the techniques and expertise brought from the great centres of Europe. What the Venetians and the Knights Hospitaller were doing in the Cyclades and the Dodecanese, the Genoese were doing even more thoroughly in Chios.

The houses of the Knights and the society of merchants and craftsmen that developed in the Dodecanese were more elaborate than elsewhere in the Aegean. They were built in terraces filling whole

The bottom half of a panel from a Rhodian bed tent, composed of four strips each containing a vertical row of coats of arms, ranging from a recognisable heraldic device on the left to a clotted blob on the right. Each panel is edged with a leaf pattern, alternately red and blue. Worked in a raised Rhodian cross stitch on heavy linen. The panels taper in width from 40 to 18 cm. Rhodes, before 1700.

blocks in the towns; they had more than one floor and the rooms were separated from each other by permanent walls and usually dedicated to a single usage, presaging the later houses of Valetta with the *piano nobile*. Within these houses there was room for more elaborate furniture, especially for a dominant bed.

When Rhodes and the neighbouring islands, particularly Kos and Karpathos, became centres of the Knights, the bed asssumed much greater importance. Following a patrician European style it now stood isolated in a dedicated room, surrounded by a bed tent rising like a conical tower up to the ceiling, where it was suspended from a round wooden plaque. This bed tent was the main decorative feature in the house, as bed curtains were elsewhere in the Aegean. Originally it may have been imported together with its woven or tapestry hangings from Europe, but gradually these were replaced by cheaper locally produced embroidered hangings. These, in turn, became richer and more elaborate, leading eventually to the very specific types of embroidered tents that have survived.

p.185

The bed tent was called a *sperveri*, the name dating from the beginning of the fifteenth century, derived, it has been suggested, from the French *épervier*, a loose-woven fishing net; I am inclined to prefer the derivation from the Italian *sparviere*, the word for both a sparrow-hawk and a bed pavilion, because the open bed tent would look like a bird in flight. Rigmor Krarup relates it to the High German *Sparwari*, and it is clearly the Middle English word *sparver*, used from the fourteenth to the end of the seventeenth century to refer to the set of textiles decorating the bed.

The sequence of development of the Rhodian sparver might have been as follows: first, a limited decoration on the panels that flanked the opening to the bed, then every front panel of the tent would be decorated, making it necessary that the opening be distinguished by more and more elaborate decoration, leading eventually to the panels being converted into doors with a quite different repertory of patterns. Gradually each panel of the bed would become more and more decorated, including internal back panels, making a blaze of colour and richness in relatively plain houses. The bed tent developed in two main forms, a Rhodian and a Koan version, both similar in shape but bearing different decorations.

The Rhodian sparver is the most spectacular of all Mediterranean furnishings: in situ it must have made a most powerful statement about the importance of the owner. Although popular tradition always associates such finery only with weddings, it is clear that these were in constant use and, from the evidence of the pieces themselves, would have been endlessly adapted to suit changing fashions. In the nineteenth century they became festival objects, associated with the past and with a skill that had disappeared; they were brought out for special occasions as part of the *mostra*, to display the wealth and standing of the family. So valuable were they that they were dismantled, divided and re-cycled. Consequently there are only about a dozen complete

A bed tent of eleven panels hung over a bed. The two door panels have decorative jambs topped by a Mamluk star, the side panels are filled with a variety of coats of arms and floral patterns, with added horizontal panels of broad-leaf and spitha and plants in vases, worked by various hands. The bed cover has been made up of separated coats of arms taken from other panels or valances joined by crochet and needle-lace strips. The tent can be stylistically attributed to Tilos, 1680-1750.

ones left, and a number of those have been patched and re-assembled with panels from other tents.

The sparver is composed of up to twelve panels and a door which is differently embroidered, either as two panels or one split up the middle. The panels that lie in front of the bed were usually densely embroidered, while those set behind were left without decoration, or were lightly embroidered on the surface facing into the bed, so that they could be seen by the occupants.

The sparver is usually between 250 and 350 cm in length, with each panel tapering from about 40-45 cm at the base to 13-17 cms at the top. The door panels also taper in early tents, but in later ones remain parallel-sided. The other panels are tapered by cutting one side only on the cross, this is then hemmed and joined to the next panel, allowing the natural selvedge to remain on the other side. This cut bias determines on which side of the door the panel is set. In most examples the decoration is contained within each panel width and consists of vertical rows of the design, scaling down in size as the pattern rises up the panel to fit in with the reduced width; the panels are then sewn edge to edge with a tight fishbone stitch. In some tents the panels are joined with narrow ribbon inserts, which I think were added when the tents were re-assembled after having been dismantled, both as a strengthening and also as an extra, but unneccesary, decoration.

p.160

The bed tent was hung from the ceiling, fixed to a wooden shield called a *milosperveri*, which was either circular or polygonal to suit the number of panels in the the tent. The *milosperveri* was either carved or painted on the surface pointing down onto the bed, usually hung from a hook, sometimes with a conical cage made of string, which was then enclosed in a cover. I know of only one cover that survives with its tent, the one at the Laing Gallery in Newcastle, part of the Bosanquet Bequest. The cage cover is 56 cm deep and 217 cm at its widest, composed of ten triangular panels sewn roughly together and lined with a coarse blue linen. The panels are made of Turkish polychrome brocade, Turkish and Persian dress brocades, Venetian yellow satin and a green Genoese damask.

The motifs used in Rhodian tents vary considerably. The basic one used on all panels except the door panels is a coat of arms with an edging of leaf shapes set sideways. The most perfect example of this type is the E.G. Howarth tent shown at the Burlington Fine Arts Club (BFAC) Exhibition in 1914, and is composed of eight panels and a separate two-panelled door which were bought together by him as one tent. The whereabouts of this bed tent is not now known, so one cannot study it. From the surviving photographs one can see that seven of the panels have a uniform pattern of eleven coats of arms with a sideways leaf-pattern edging; the eighth panel has no centre pattern and must therefore have been the panel set to the wall.

There are two patterns used on the door panels, either with or without a gable. The first, without gable, consists in each half, bottom to top, of a row of leaves set sideways, a large coat of arms with

Left A bed tent hanging over a bed, composed of a door panel, seven front panels and five back panels. The door panel has a Mamluk star in the gable and peacocks above it. The front is all coats of arms while the back has small vases. Above the bed tent there is a rare contemporary dust cover, made of panels of brocade and velvet. Bought by Bosanquet in 1902. Rhodes, before 1700.

Above A panel of three rows of the double-leaf pattern worked very densely. These panels are usually placed above the door gable in Rhodian bed tents and occasionally flanking the lower part of the door. Rhodes, before 1750.

supporters and three horizontal rows of a broad-leaf pattern separated by stripes of a geometric pattern. All the space left is filled with seven-legged animals and irregular blocks of colour, then four coats of arms similar to those in the side panels set one above the other, with the last one intruding into a frieze which must have been added later. Above the frieze there are two more rows of the same broad-leaf pattern, of which there are three rows lower down. The frieze, which allows one to classify the type, is composed of a central eight-pointed star, a Mamluk motif, set with six smaller eight-pointed stars about it, flanked by a pair of peacocks, then the head of the intruding coats of arms and a final two-headed eagle pattern. The background is filled with small animals and simplified coats of arms.

This basic pattern changed over time, but the three panels of horizontal pattern placed low on the door were preserved even when the door shape changed. This can be seen in both the Benaki and the Bosanquet beds: the panels have been sewn onto the panels flanking the bought-in door, covering areas that have not been embroidered.

The side panels are embroidered alternately in green and red, but the door additionally has black, yellow and a little blue-green. The sparver in the Washington Textile Museum has a door identical to the Howarth door, but the V&A Museum piece is a composite of side panels from three separate tents, and the tent door is unusual in that it follows a later development than the Howarth tent, with the frieze as part of the original design. It has the Mamluk star and the pair of opposed peacocks but with a filling of a very sparse sprig pattern. The door panels, instead of having a column of the coat of arms pattern, have a column of five water ewers of various sizes topped by a Mamluk eight-pointed medallion. The pieces in the Cook collection are very similar to the Howarth piece, except that the central star and peacock are flanked by the Mamluk medallion found in the Washington tent, and the supporters to the coats of arms have become separated from their arms and stand upright alone.

The second type of the Rhodian tent differs in that the panels of the tent contain a wider range of patterns; the edging leaf pattern is very heavy and solid, worked in a coarser and fatter stitch. The patterns range from three types of the coats of arms, becoming less and less well defined, and a vase shape, the *glastra*, and a *dixos* are introduced. The glastra shape is derived from a flat-bottomed or footed vase, from the classic Greek *glastron*. The dixos is a round filled shape very reminiscent of an Islamic pattern. I have been unable to relate the word to a classic word and reject the idea that it is an inverted form of the word disc, which would have simplified the problem.

This second type is best exemplified by the De Dino tent in the Metropolitan Museum, where the side panels are composed of patterns which are not coats of arms but combinations of vases, medallions and branch patterns, all set within each panel and edged on three sides by the slanted leaf pattern. This tent is composed of 17½ panels in all, 15½ side panels, split 7½ on the left and 8 on the right, and 2 door panels; 4½ panels on the right and 5 on the left carry the conventional design of a central column flanked by leaves. In this case the pattern on the first panel is a branch pattern and the others are all vases set on little feet. The remaining 6 panels, 3 on each side, are fully embroidered with medallions of three different shapes with leaf borders. The door is of the first type but includes a gable. I am inclined to believe that this tent is composed of side panels from two separate sets of bed furnishings. The combination of the total 17½ panels makes the tent far larger and more important than a bed furnishing, in so much that when it was exhibited as part of the Arms and Armoury Collection at the Metropolitan, before it was transferred to the Textile Department, it was presented as a Military tent of the fifteenth or early sixteenth century made in Cyprus, which followed the description in the catalogue of the De Dino Collection made in 1901 by Baron C.A. de Cosson. It is there incorrectly compared to a tent in the Real Armeria in Madrid, which is an Ottoman campaign tent.

The bed tent which belonged to Professor Felix von Luschan of Berlin University is composed of twelve panels plus two door panels. It is unusual in that the twelve panels are embroidered with a range of very simplified coats of arms, almost reducing the pattern to a basic glastra. The only existing illustration of this tent shows that the stitch used is not the thick Rhodian cross stitch but a simpler single cross stitch, associated with some of the other Dodecanese Islands, and if that were so then the provenance and date of the piece would have to be reconsidered. Professor von Luschan placed the tent as having been made before the flight of the Knights from Rhodes in 1522. If that is so then the piece is unique. However, from the pattern and style I would place it at the earliest at about 1750. This tent was sold to a

Prospetto di casa lindiota.

Above A view of the priest Constantine's house in Lindos showing the complicated door gables copied in the embroidered bed tents. La Città Sacra.

Right The upper part of the door panel of a bed tent from Kos. This single panel was made separately and added to any form of bed tent. The single gable contains plants and birds but the area above, the museo, contains a range of heraldic emblems, galleons, a lady in a castle, little humans and birds. (Plate 45 in *Mediterranean and Near East Embroideries*, 1935.) About 1700.

collector in America in 1926 and has since been lost, as has the other tent that belonged to Count Charles Lanckoroniki.

The Wace bed tent now at Liverpool is of this second type, and composed of twenty panels, all tapering and 330 cm long. The ten panels in the front are embroidered and the ten at the back are all blank. This is the most complete of all the existent tents and most likely in its original state. It has no special door; there is merely a slit between the third and fourth panels with a border running up the jamb to identify the entrance. The three panels on each side of the slit have a pattern of tree and branch variants; the next four panels on the right each have a different pattern, 12 to 14 repeats of each in the panel. The sequence is a stylized double-headed eagle, a glastra on a tall foot, a glastra with two handles, a skeletal tree with trefoil flowers, and the last a variant of the glastra, all worked in the heavy cross stitch in alternate red and green. By the beginning of the nineteenth century these designs had deteriorated into solid rectangular blobs and it is only by observing the way in which the fat cross stitch is laid that one sees vestiges of the original coat of arms or vase.

p.178

The second type of Rhodian door, used with the same sets of side panels, has the total ground covered in a dense blocking of the broad leaf with infills of coloured blocks, all embroidered in the raised cross stitch in polychrome. A gable is first introduced with the triangular shape on the outer edge of the vertical jambs, but the inner jambs of the gable ascend straight into the tympanum without being joined in any way. The von Luschan tent door, which does not belong to the tent, introduces a triangle on top of the inner jambs which fits snugly into the eight-pointed Mamluk star.

The area above the gable is called *koumpaso*, the name derived from the medieval Italian word for that shape defined by the arms of a pair of compasses. It is usually filled with a pair of opposed birds, either peacocks or cockerels, stylized blocks of double eagles, and irregular blocks of colour. It may be, as in the Luschan tent, that the door was only ever about two-thirds the length of the tent and that the koumpaso was never entirely filled with embroidery, allowing it to be joined to any size of tent, hence occasionally needing the straight panel at the top of the door to fill in what would otherwise be an unacceptable blank. An interesting feature is the different form of the main pair of opposed birds in these doors; they come, most commonly, with curved upright tails, with straight upright tails or with straight downward tails.

The third type of Rhodian tent is quite different to the preceding two in that the curtain is first assembled with all the panels sewn together, and then completely over-embroidered with the pattern worked over the seams. The pattern is usually a variant of a small glastra, and only the outside edge of the whole curtain leaf of three of four joined widths carries the edging pattern of leaves set sideways. The patterns are set out in ascending columns, with a half drop between rows, the patterns reducing in size to allow them to fit into the

narrowing panels. The embroidery is worked in a thick cross stitch and usually in three colours – a strong red, a soft green and a soft blue.

This type of bed tent has been reported by travellers in Rhodes, Tilos, Nisyros and Chalki, but none have been reported from Astypalaia, Kasos or Karpathos, although most certainly bed curtains would have been made there to fit a different style of bed.

It becomes clear as one studies the Rhodian bed tents that they were professional rather than domestic products, especially the doors, which must have been the product of ateliers in Rhodes. They were probably made to order, incorporating the patterns required, and because they were to fit side panels made elsewhere they were left rectangular and not tapered, and made to a standard height and then cut or augmented to fit the tent. Not only were these doors atelier work, but I believe that doors for the other bed tents in the Dodecanese, to be described later, were also professional products and may even have been made in Rhodes for export.

The bed tents are displayed in museums accompanied by an embroidered valance, all made of two strips of linen sewn horizontally, selvedge to selvedge, to form a panel 165-280 cm long and, where both panels are still joined, 100 cm deep. The bottom strip usually has a row of seven or nine of the main motif surrounded by a leaf-pattern edging. The top strip has only a bottom edging of the leaf pattern, with the rest of the top undecorated, indicating that the rest of the top panel would not be seen, presumably because it was tucked under a mattress. The fall of the tent would mean that most of the embroidery of the valance, if it was used in that way, would not be seen, which is quite contrary to the way in which the embroideries were used. If valances were used as a pelmet at the top of bed curtains to cover the gap between the curtain and the ceiling, as they do in the Cyclades, it is not the case in the Dodecanese: the bed furnishings do not require it. It is more likely that the matching valances were used elsewhere in the room, either as a spare bed or bench cover, or they may have been hung over cassone or simpler undecorated boxes used for storing clothing. This would be more in keeping with contemporary Italian fashion.

There are more valances left than bed tents, and many of them have been attributed, quite rightly I think, to Kasos and Karpathos, where there is no tradition of the bed tent and certainly no surviving examples. These long valances are easily adapted and have often been reshaped and re-cycled, sometimes with added embroidery, which is quite alien to the original style, and sometimes using wool in a chain stitch or even a simple stem stitch.

p.82, 83, 150

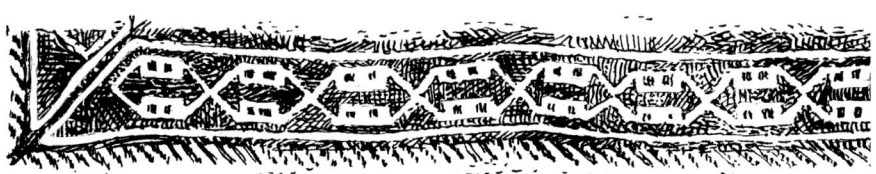

Kos

Kos, the second seat of the Knights, was their military centre between 1306 and 1522, from where they controlled their land on the opposite Turkish coast. It was held in rotation by different Tongues from Rhodes that all helped build the castle and the large town houses. Kos was the ancient name but during the period of the Knights it was known as Lango or Stanchio, a corruption of the Greek phrase *eis tin Ko*.

Inevitably, Kos followed the fashions of Rhodes but developed its own decorative vocabulary. The main difference is that Koan work, particularly the early work, uses a fine single darning stitch instead of the heavy cross stitch. Koan textiles were therefore much lighter and so the weight of the embroidery did not cause the textiles to tear or deteriorate so easily; consequently far more work has survived. Koan embroiderers used some of the Rhodian designs but changed them substantially, introducing the *dixos* pattern into both their own work and to that of the neighbouring islands.

The bed had the same importance as in Rhodes, but the furnishings used with it developed differently. One version has the form of the Rhodian sparver for a free-standing bed, the other continues an older tradition, already observed in the Cyclades, of the bed in an alcove. Very similar bed furnishings to those from Kos may also have come from Nisyros, Tilos or Symi; there are references in the literature to all these islands having bed tents; Dawkins refers to a bed tent in a doctor's house in Tilos that had a door similar to the one in Newcastle.

Two basic patterns are used on the bed tent. The most common one is an elaboration of the branch pattern, *spitha*, the other is the *dixos*, of which there is a large number of variants. The dixos is found in both the long bed tents and the shorter bed curtains, and is not exclusive to Kos but would have been used in all the islands of the eastern Dodecanese, extensively in Nisyros and in Astypalaia, where it also appears on the large sleeves of the women's costume.

The spitha pattern is basically a broad chevron composed of nine square blocks, one at the apex and four in each arm. The blocks are alternately patterned as a chequerboard and a square filled with a small angular dog. The internal angle of the chevron has yet another dog and above it a pair of opposed fat birds with vestigal wings set about a small diamond, which is filled with a swastika or fylfot. Above this diamond rises the basic spitha with latch-hooked arms and a branched tree shape above it. Tree or large leaf shapes rise from the end of the chevron in two directions. A row of feathered latch hooks depend from the lower edge of the chevron, with a feathered diamond chequerboard as a pendant finial. The only variant to this basic pattern that I know of is only a change in scale; the arms of this version are much narrower and are composed of eleven squares with the angular dog replaced by a windmill sail, or with a small 'S' shape. Both versions of the spitha are found in the same bed tent, sometimes even on the same panel. It is always embroidered in the centre of each panel, repeated for the whole length and only varied in colour. Each spitha is of one colour only and, as always, red predominates, but is alternated with blue, green or gold versions. The vertical rows are edged on both sides with isolated repeats of an eight-pointed star pattern, of which I have identified three basic versions. The similarity of this basic spitha shape to Mamluk embroidery has already been noted.

The dixos is essentially a medallion derived from Eastern textiles, like the *gul* pattern found in so many carpets and embroideries from Turkey and Persia. The shape of the medallion varies considerably and is another splendid example of how a simple basic pattern has been developed and elaborated by the genius of the embroiderer. The dixos is always embroidered in one colour only, unlike the the glastra, which can be two-coloured. It is found in both versions of the bed furnishing; on the sparver it follows the Rhodian style, but on the bed curtains it is usually set out in the same way as the spitha, a series of five or six repeats placed upright vertically within a border of a variety of roundels and squares, similar in style to the edging used for the bed tents. The design is contained within each panel, which were embroidered separately and then joined selvedge to selvedge to make the curtain leaves, accounting for the irregularities in the completed curtain. These curtains are the simplest of all the embroideries, and because of their oblong regular shape have been recycled to be used as bedspreads and hangings once the need for them as bed curtains ended.

The named varieties of the dixos that I have come across are: *stronghilos* – round, *koskinatos* – like a sieve, *amygdalatos* – almond shaped, *caridato* – walnut shaped, *apidato* – pear shaped, *kladeftiri* – with branches, *gigliato* – with lilies, *carrafillia* – with carnations, *astrudachia* – with stars, *patiniotiko* – from Patmos, *cotiko* – from Kos, *maidato* – with a Turkish

Left A sleeve with nine dixos of the peach leaf pattern edged on two sides with an Italian renaissance wreath border. Leros, about 1720.

Right A bed tent from Kos. The tent is composed of nine panels, each with a rising column of the spitha pattern, garded to fit the taper with edges of a Mamluk star. The door panel has columns of broad-leaf and spitha within the first gable, the second has two-headed eagles, birds and flowering branches. The museo above has the two-headed eagle and pairs of dragons, birds and leopards. The door is topped by two horizontal panels of the pattern within the door jambs. About 1700.

coin, 'maide', *papamichalati* – Father Michael's pattern, *me perdikes* – with partridges.

The doors for the sparvers from Kos and the other Dodecanese islands are as splendid as the Rhodian ones They differ in style but must also have been made professionally. They could have been incorporated into a bed tent that may have been made domestically, although even those are likely to have been made by professionals. Koan doors are of a very particular type, apparently more expensive than the Rhodian version, using finer embroidery on a heavier linen. This would support the idea of professional ateliers producing them, most probably in the Chora of Kos, although they may have been made in Lindos on Rhodes, for which there are many references of professional embroiderers working.

The door has wide jambs filled with alternate broad leaf and spitha patterns packed densely on top of each other in rising columns into a gable, which often has the same pattern in it. The area above the gable, the koumpaso, is filled with a wild variety of invented and fantastic motifs. Although the word koumpaso was used into the first decade of this century, the word now used for the area above the gable is *mouseion*, the museum, because of the range of strange beasts found in it. The inspiration for this menagerie is quite varied: from the Byzantine ecclesiastical and military traditions come the opposed birds, the double-headed eagles and the sailing vessels; from Mamluk Egypt come the deer, parrots, leopards and the eight-pointed stars; from Europe via Venice come the heraldic lions in a number of versions and the stylized embroidery infills, and finally from the native spirit come the little human beings, the fantastic, mythological figures and the simplified versions of other patterns.

There are a number of versions of the gables themselves, both in their number, in the way that they are structurally placed and the decorations that surround them. The various versions are: without a gable, with an isolated gable, one gable, two gables and finally three. The Honolulu Academy of Arts has a curtain with a door which has only a pair of parrots in the koumpaso, the Royal Ontario Museum door has the parrots as well as an infill of smaller stylized birds. Both these doors are very short and topped by panels cut from other tents. One can only speculate why this variety exists; it was not done to compensate for varying heights of the tents, as the doors were all of about the same height irrespective of the number of gables introduced; it may just be another example of the belief that 'more is better'. Many of the bought doors which would have been of standard lengths were shortened to fit the side panels, and later altered to satisfy changing fashions. When the doors were not as long as the side panels with which they were to be used, a strip of another panel was placed above the door to compensate for that difference in height. This additional panel is usually of the Rhodian broad-leaf pattern.

I am persuaded that the embroidered gable and multiple gables are derived from architecture: there are many examples in Rhodes and

p.62

elsewhere in the Dodecanese of carved stone gateways that incorporate more than one gable; the single gable of St John's Gate in Rhodes, and the double and multiple gables of the houses in Lindos, where the space between the two gables is filled with carved patterns very similar to the embroideries in the koumpaso.

Apart from the shape of the door gables, it is also possible to identify the various doors by a particular motif used in the koumpaso. They all, with the exception of the Honolulu and Ontario curtains mentioned earlier, have in the koumpaso a collection of birds, deer, leafy branches and small rosettes, with some very distinctive motifs such as a figure in p.78 a small tower, lions, blue double-headed eagles and sailing vessels, which are called *dilinia* in Greek, from the Italian *vascelli di linea,* or *karavia,* again from the Italian *caravella,* as part of the elaborate decoration.

These doors are used with the spitha curtains, and even with others where they are not so appropriate. Presumably the bought-in doors from Kos were found to be so attractive that they were added to tents throughout the islands to enhance their value and to bring them up to fashion. When they did not fit they were augmented by patches from other furnishings placed above the gable.

The same patterns were used throughout the area, and many examples from after 1850 have survived from Kos which are invariably decorated with the dixos, but these late examples are worked in a tight cross stitch, maintaining the tradition of alternating colours, red and green or red and blue.

Variations of the spitha pattern have survived, as have different versions of the edging pattern. There is a sufficient difference between these three variants to allow us to speculate that they may have been produced in one of the other islands, perhaps Leros or Kalymnos.

The front panel from a poukamiso decorated with six galleons in full sail, with riders on large birds on the decks. Astypalaia, about 1720.

Patmos

Patmos is the northernmost of the Dodecanese, renowned for the Monastery of St John, which was founded by the saintly Christodoulos in 1088 on the site of the cave where St John is said to have written the Book of Revelations. Richard Pococke, in 1745, said that there were 300 churches on Patmos; in 1817 Walpole said there were 240 and that each one was used only on the festival day of its patronal saint. The population of Patmos has always been very small and has been dedicated to the church. Consequently there have been very few women other than nuns on the island.

A central problem with the so-called Patmian embroideries is the critical one as to whether any at all were made on Patmos. The original attribution was made by Wace with no supporting evidence, and there are no details of his collecting in the island; Dawkins only once mentions another embroidery in his note book as having a stitch similar to a Patmian stitch. It is only in the first catalogue of the Fitzwilliam Exhibition in 1905 that three pieces are referred to as being from 'Patmos District in a Patmian stitch', and another Naxian piece is described as having a Patmian stitch. Three stitches are used in this work, but it must be the small darning stitch, almost a stem stitch, that is meant by this 'Patmian stitch'. Perhaps the intention was to emphasise that it was not the heavy cross stitch of Rhodes. By the time of the BFAC Exhibition in 1914 the attribution to Patmos becomes fixed and all the pieces which are worked exclusively in the broad-leaf p.146 pattern are attributed to Patmos, whereas today one would be inclined to suggest the Cyclades as the provenance, and would relate them stylistically to the south-eastern islands.

The textiles that are today called Patmos, almost entirely as a consequence of Wace's original attribution, are amongst the oldest that have survived. They have the appearance of being older than all the Koan pieces and certainly rival the earliest versions of the Rhodian curtains; they are contemporary with the Cycladic Melos curtains, reinforcing my opinion of their origin.

The only pattern used in this group of embroideries is a column of alternating broad leaf and spitha patterns. Both patterns are treated as p.24 blocks and are set one on top of another to fit as closely into each other as is possible, even if this requires some portion of the pattern to be lost. In some versions of this design a pair of small opposed dogs is set above the spitha, so as to fit into the space left by the upward curve of the next broad leaf. In another version the small dogs are replaced by either a pair of prancing opposed birds or a pair of erect heraldic lions, but in exactly the same position in the design, filling the space between the two motifs.

The design is placed on each panel in columns in a half-drop, so that the two motifs alternate in both directions, allowing each pattern to be read diagonally, although the half-drop is not always accurate. The columns of the two alternating patterns are placed so as to lie within the strip of each panel, and are invariably bordered with a band of a geometric pattern edged on both sides by a small triangular floral frieze, of which there are three main versions. This border is also used in the bed panels and doors to separate each column of the main design, both horizontally and vertically. The same border pattern is also found in the doors that usually accompany the Koan bed tents.

These embroideries all come from curtains to be used with an alcove bed. They were composed of eight panels, divided into two curtains of four panels each, hung on either side of the door. Each curtain, including the door panels, is 200 cm in width and between 270 and 300 cm in length. Each panel would be totally covered with embroidery in three columns of the one pattern, edged with the banded border on both sides and the bottom. The embroidery would be taken almost to the top of the curtain, sometimes with an extra motif added at the top of the central column so as to give a crenallated effect. The two panels which are used to differentiate the side panels from the entrance to the bed are embroidered in exactly the same pattern, with the three columns in each leaf of the door leading up to a single or double gable.

Later the door panels are distinguished by having the original three columns set above two or three horizontal rows of the same pattern, separated horizontally by bands of the same border, so as to give the effect of a separate valance. The design in the horizontal rows of this false valance differs from the vertical pattern by alternating the standard broad leaf with the spitha above it, with two smaller broad-leaf patterns set one above the other. Even these curtains are furnished with the imported Koan or Rhodian doors.

p.61

If the embroideries were made in Patmos then it is difficult to think who might have made or used them. They are almost exclusively bed curtains and clearly secular in use, with no now discernible eccleciastical use. I cannot imagine the Hiegoumenos allowing them around his bed or authorising the monks, who formed over half the population of the island, to make them. The problem then becomes one of deciding where they do come from if not from Patmos. They are all of one specific type; they belong to the bed in an alcove or set on a sofa, they do not taper, and are generally the size of the standard Cycladic curtain, and in style bear the greatest resemblance to the curtains from Amorgos. Like those curtains they are worked in polychrome silk on a fine linen, but the quality of the work is far superior to that of Amorgos, but unlike the Amorgos curtains, that only use darning stitch, these curtains use satin stitch and a very tight chain stitch as well. We must wait for more research to discover the answer.

Kalymnos and Nisyros

Kalymnos lies just north of Kos, some ten miles west of the Turkish coast, opposite ancient Halicarnassos. It is the home of the many sponge fishers who left every year for the north African coast. The island does not have a reputation for embroidery: most of those pieces that are left which are attributed to the island are the dresses, the first of which was collected by W.R.Paton in Kalymnos before 1885, while carrying out a dig there for the Royal Hellenic Society. He gave his two dresses to the V&A Museum in 1887. Others of the same period are in the Ashmolean Museum and in private collections. The poukamisos are of the oriental Byzantine cut, made up of straight lengths of linen weave which have two or three stripes of silk or cotton warps along the selvedge ends as decoration. The embroidery is confined to the front skirt, the sleeve ends and a little around the long neck opening. Occasionally the short sleeves have long hanging sleeve-ends attached, made of a striped Turkish silk. A tradition in the island was that a new bride took with her dresses that she had embroidered but never worn. The neck opening would not even be cut, the dress known as *akopti*, and then after the marriage her new sisters-in-law would cut the neck opeing, as a symbol of the wedding, and then embroider it themselves. This would account for the difference in design and hand often seen between the main embroidery and the neck opening.

The patterns are very Turkish, being forms of flowers and leaves on a pole or in a vase, and have some affinity to the dixos patterns found in Kos and neighbouring Leros. The work is meticulously done in coloured silks, in cross, satin, feather and double running stitches in a large range of colours, and is very distinctively outlined in black, which is particular to them.

The only pieces other than the dresses that are attributed to Kalymnos are the remnants of curtains, a valance and a large spread, but with no justification at all. The work in these pieces is fairly coarse, both in the quality of the base linen fabric and the execution of the embroidery - a loose darning and double running stitch - and would not appear to have come from the same tradition as the dresses. The pattern is always a unit of a branch and leaves set diagonally and outlined in black. However, the valance is of much finer work and is very similar to the poukamisos.

It is difficult to ascribe a distinctive tradition to Kalymnos, and if Paton had not collected his dresses there - which may easily have come from the Greeks on the Turkish coast - then no embroidery would be attributed to the island at all.

A poukamiso from Kalymnos, the front and sleeves decorated with a stylized bunch of flowers and leaves. Long tasselled sleeves of striped Turkish silk have been added. The poukamiso is unfinished, the neck uncut, and this would have been part of a dowry, to be completed after the marriage in the new house, where it would have been embroidered by the new sisters-in law. Collected in 1890. About 1820.

The small islands of Nisyros, Tilos, Symi and Leros lie north of Rhodes, clustered around Kos, and like it their history is bound to the Hospitaller Knights. The Knights administered and repopulated them, building castles and houses there before they fell to the Turks, together with Rhodes, in 1522. Fantino Querini, who was related to the Lords of Astypalaia and who had become a Knight Hospitaller, was appointed as controller of Nisyros in 1433. During his rule a large number of families was moved between the islands, which may account for the many similarities between the costume and embroidery styles of the different islands.

Some embroideries have been tentatively attributed to these islands; travellers referred to having seen embroideries there, and some collectors have labelled pieces that they bought on the islands as having been made there. Unfortunately there is no guarantee that they were in fact made there. Both bed tents and curtains were used, but they would have been imported rather than made on the islands. Some valances and cushions are attributed to them, but without any supporting evidence. The style in these islands is Koan, and any

Rhodian motifs used are altered to local versions, as can be seen in a tent panel and two almost identical valances at the V&A Museum which use a version of the vase and glastra - it is quite different to anything else in the Dodecanese, with small edging designs which are quite unique.

The best known embroideries attributed to Nisyros are the women's costumes. An assumption that may be made is that even the poorer islands, which did not make bed furnishings, would still decorate formal costume. Perhaps it is now appropriate to discuss the range of women's dresses common in the Dodecanese.

The islands where embroidery on clothing is of great importance are Nisyros, Astypalaia, Kasos and Karpathos, or rather one should say that the few embroidered garments that have survived are from these remoter islands. Perhaps the conclusion one should draw is that, like provinces and even cities on the mainland, originally every island had a tradition of embroidered garments, but that it survived longer in the remoter islands. Certainly the islands that were more vistied, and where foreign influence was greater, more quickly abandoned domestic embroidery, using imported woven and printed decorated fabrics instead of a local product. This is evident in the engraved prints of the area: in the middle of the eighteenth century the ladies of the larger islands are shown wearing imported fashions, whereas prints of the nineteenth century from Kasos and Karpathos still show women wearing their traditional embroidered dresses.

The embroidery worked on garments is usually on the women's clothes. It is the accepted view that these lavishly embroidered garments were kept for special occasions, but it is clear that originally even everyday clothes were decorated; it was only later that they became heirlooms and were kept without being worn at all. There is very little evidence of embroidery on the men's costume; if decorated it was fairly simple: usually a black band at the collar or sleeve.

The embroidered dresses were the *poukamiso*, derived either from the Byzantine garment of the same name or the later Italianate renaissance dress. The poukamiso was itself merely a version of the tunic shift universally worn by both men and women in the Near East from ancient times. It is made from straight lengths of a fabric, using the whole of the loom width; the front and back are of one continuous length with a cut neck opening. A long triangular piece, usually a loom width cut diagonally, is inserted on each side to make a flare. Sleeves are added to the shoulder in a straight line; quite the simplest way to create a garment, avoiding any tailoring. Sleeves are short and broad and stand out from the body of the dress. The island poukamiso is a version of this Byzantine garment with a slightly more flared tunic and square-cut sleeves inset at the shoulder. The neck opening is straight cut, hemmed or turned back and edged with a small band making a narrow collar.

The other version is the 'European cut' and is made up of a wide skirt gathered at the waist and a bodice with full sleeves gathered at the shoulders. The sleeves are usually wrist length, although some only

A poukamiso from Rhodes cut in the Byzantine style with clotted black and blue embroidery on the skirt and sleeve borders. The long neck opening has been worked in a different design by another hand. About 1750.

reach to the mid-forearm. This is a renaissance dress style from Italy and the outstanding feature of it, as can be seen from many renaissance portraits, is the heavily decorated full sleeve.

The Byzantine poukamiso was worn in Rhodes, Karpathos and Kasos and, with some variation in cut, it must have been worn in all the islands along the Turkish coast. The decoration on the Rhodian dresses was mainly along the hem and at the end of the sleeves, with very simple stitching at the neck. In a Rhodian dress the skirt border is usually 8 cm wide, worked in the thick Rhodian cross stitch in black, with a thin edging of blue. The pattern is so clotted as to be impossible to describe; it is very similar in feeling to the last stage of pattern development on the Rhodian bed tent, when the coats of arms or glastras become rectangular blobs worked very tightly, with all sense of the original inspiration having been lost. A simpler version is composed of a row of isolated circular filled shapes in alternating colours, set around the hem, rather in the same style as the cushions.

p.150

The varieties of decoration on the two main dress styles will be described with the other embroideries from each island.

Astypalaia

Astypalaia is a remote small island which, because of its position, had a certain importance in antiquity. During the Frankish empire of Greece it was part of the Duchy of Naxos and was given in 1207, together with some other islands, to Giovanni Querini, whose family continued to own it until 1537. On behalf of Venice the Querini administered other islands in the Aegean, amongst them Amorgos, Tinos and Mykonos and later, through Fantino, they controlled Nisyros, Kalymnos and Leros in the Dodecanese. Astypalaia was sacked by Omar, Bey of Aidin, in 1341

A sleeve from a Nisyros poukamiso in the pattern called vetses, the earrings, with an Italianate wreath border. The shoulder and upper seams are worked with polychrome hexagons and roses with a little metal thread. About 1750.

but the Querini stayed on and later shared the island with the Grimani.

Astypalaia, Karpathos and Kasos were known as the Venetian Islands and were always very closely supervised by Venice through the Querini, who abandoned them to the Turks after the Franco-Turkish treaty of 1536, which had as one of its main terms that the French would help oust the Venetians from the Aegean. Astypalaia had been deserted and repopulated by various rulers, and in 1540 it was reported that all the inhabitants had fled to Crete. The island was repopulated in the following years by peoples from the neighbouring islands, and by Albanians being moved there from other Cycladic islands where they had been installed earlier. One understands 'Albanians' to mean any of the mainland populations that slowly moved or were moved into the islands; it is unlikely that there were that many actual Albanians available to be moved about at this time.

The Querini were so taken with their possession of Astypalaia that they took to calling themselves Querini-Stampalia, and their home in Venice was called the Palazzo Querini-Stampalia, which since 1868 has been a library and picture galllery housing the family collection. After the Turkish occupation Astypalaia was administered from Rhodes, and when the new Kingdom of Greece was created in 1832, even though the Cyclades were part of Greece and Astypalaia had been captured by the Greeks during the War of Independence in 1821, it was returned to the Turks in exchange for total rights to Euboea. It did not become part of Greece until 1947, when it was ceded by Italy together with the other Dodecanese islands.

The embroidery of Astypalaia shares two traditions, one derived from its connection with the Duchy and the second with its later incorporation into the Dodecanese. Because of its relative isolation it preserved a local tradition of embroidery, which was mainly used to decorate women's costume and for special ceremonial cloths made for weddings and christenings. There are no pieces which I can identify as being part of the expected bed furnishings, although Marica Monte Santo, a great ethnologist, does mention sheets. The bed was set in a raised alcove at one end of the simple single-roomed house, reached by a box set as a step in front of it. There is no history of either curtains or tents; the household embroideries that have survived are towels and shelf cloths.

The costume of Astypalaia is a fusion of Byzantium, Venice and the East, and the Astypalaian woman dressed in her full festival costume appears like a figure out of Imperial Byzantium. The European cut dress, with its large, billowing sleeves, was the usual one in Astypalaia, and very similar versions of it were worn in Nisyros and Tilos. The dresses are well known because of the work of Marica Monte Santo, who was commissioned by the Italian Ministry of the Colonies to

An Astypalaian lady wearing the costume called zatouni, the skirt embroidered with partridges, the sleeves with stripes, the head-cloth with flowers. She is wearing the skoufia on her head, draped with the chrysomandilo. Photograph taken in 1929, the embroideries dating from a century earlier. Astypalaia.

study the island as part of the series of studies of the colonies in the early 1930s. She published her work as *L'Isola dei Gigli* in 1932, at which time there was enough of the old life still to be studied; sadly it has now disappeared altogether. The costumes of Nisyros, Tilos and Chalki are similar in one respect or another, and from the surviving examples one assumes that the Astypalaian version represents the oldest and most complete tradition.

There are two versions of this European cut dress, both based on a similar body but with different sleeves attached to it. The first has the top of the large linen sleeves quilled onto the yoke of the bodice with either a wide bar of embroidery or an added band of narrow braiding, set over a strip of woollen fabric. The second version has the sleeve sewn onto the yoke with the gathering necessary to accommodate it. Both of these attachment methods act as a reinforcement to hold up sleeves heavy with embroidery. The pattern on both versions of these sleeves can be either stripes or an arrangement of large dixos.

p.66, 75

The stripes are arranged in vertical rows, alternately narrow and wide, filling the whole sleeve. The narrow stripe is composed of a small pattern which is seen locally as a centipede, the demotic word for which is *skolopendra*, and this type of costume is therefore called *skolopendrata*. The wide vertical stripe is called *vetzes*, which is a running linked pattern. The only derivation that I have been given for this word is *vezzo*, as the word is rendered in medieval Italian, which is the name of a Greek dance where men and women hold hands and circle each other. Sometimes the stripe of the centipede pattern is replaced with a vertical row of eight-pointed stars called *maidatos*, from the name of a small Turkish coin, *maïde*, which has a Mamluk eight-pointed star on it. The sleeve is finished with a wide embroidered band composed of an Italianate leafy wreath, edged with an unbalanced star on both sides.

This type of sleeve is also found in Nisyros, and there the stripes are quite dense. The pattern which is seen in Astypalaia as a centipede is there described as either little fishes or as beetles.

The second version of the costume is the *skleta*, where the sleeve is full but decorated with versions of the dixos motif alone. Each dixos is monochrome but the diagonal rows can be in two or three colours. Again the finish of the sleeve is the same as the skolopendrata.

In both versions the skirt, *kormi*, is made of four loom widths of linen and decorated around the base with motifs that we must assume are patterns derived from the Cyclades, but developed uniquely in Astypalaia. The band of embroidery is worked along the bottom edge of each panel and rises for one pattern width up both sides of each panel. This creates a frieze running all along the bottom of the skirt, with extra decoration rising up at four places. There are many examples of such an effect on mainland Greek skirts, although there it is achieved differently.

The patterns include a pair of opposed large-tailed crowned stylised birds, called *perdikes zervodexies,* the right and left-facing partridges, alternating with a standing branch. The tail of the bird usually has a

cross embroidered in a contrasting colour on it; There are also rows of camel-like animals each with a rider on top facing the front, a single-masted galleon with two sailors alternating with a long-tailed four-legged beast; a three-masted galleon, again with little sailors set in the rigging, alternating with a mounted donkey-like animal, and finally a simplified double-headed eagle alternating with a triangular spray of leaves. The hem is finished with a continuous band of squares in different colours.

The stitches used are varied, emphasising the different traditions and cultures that are found in Astypalaia. The most interesting stitch of all is a cross stitch that looks like the Rhodian heavy cross stitch, but which in fact is a cross stitch worked as a floating surface stitch on to a pre-laid ground stitch. The process must have been to outline the pattern with a series of the first half of a cross stitch, using cotton thread, changing the direction of the laid stitch to indicate the final shape, and then to work the second arm of the cross stitch loosely in a thick flossed silk on to the first arm, without piercing the base material. This gives a slightly domed raised stitch, which may have been used more extensively in Rhodes than has been previously accepted. In addition to this floating cross stitch we find cross stitch, satin stitch, double and single darning stitches, stem stitch, long-armed cross stitch and button hole and blanket stitch at the hems. The embroidery on the sleeves of both types of dress is worked in a cross stitch, lighter than the Rhodian version, and long-armed cross stitch. The skirt borders are worked in cross stitch, back stitch and buttonhole stitch. The silk used is slightly twisted in black, blue, green or red, sometimes relieved with a metallic thread.

The range of colours used on skirts is wider than elsewhere, and although predominantly red and black other colours are also used: dark and light blue, green, ochre and lemon-yellow, orange, pink, bright cerise, purple-black and soft gold. The colours on the sleeves are more limited: green, blue and red for the dixos, and dark green, black and blue for the vertical lines of pattern. Whether particular sleeves were made for one skirt or not is now difficult to tell; in the remaining complete dresses, mainly at Liverpool, there is no observable unity in colour or design, and one is left with the impression that the more

The front panels of poukamisos, Astypalaia, about 1800. *Left* Embroidered with a frieze of double-headed eagles, with a needle-weave gusset, and *above* Embroidered with galleons with three sailors in the rigging, alternating with a man in Turkish costume riding a horse.

p.168

78

important vivid sleeves were attached to various skirts as needed.

In addition to the dresses, there is a number of embroidered pieces of costume that are unique to Astypalaia. The most important is the complicated head dress, the *skoufia*, a domed triangular cap of satin or velvet embroidered with pearls, semi-precious stones and gold wire. It is worked with a variety of patterns, mainly a central medallion flanked by shapes that may originally have been doves. Around the head band of the skoufia is fixed the *chrysomandilo*, the gold kerchief, which in fact is not a kerchief at all but a broad band of silk, sewn onto a linen backing, which lies along the forehead making an entablature. This chrysomandilo is embroidered in gold wire and set with pearls, making it the most valuable of all the pieces in the costume. The pattern is composed of three rows of animals and figures, each row surrounded with a gold braid; the rows are filled with double-headed eagles, birds, lions, curly tailed deer and stylized human figures.

The last piece of the ensemble is the cloth worn over the whole head dress, leaving the chrysomandilo visible then falling over the shoulders from the crown of the skoufia. This cloth is called an *embolia* when only the two ends are embroidered, and *machramas* or *panomustachia* when the decoration runs around all four sides. Both the embolia and the machramas are usually double-faced, a rarity in Aegean work, made of fine cotton and embroidered with a repeat of floral or vegetal forms. The whole head costume then has a set of silver jewellery attached to it called the *armatossia*, composed of multiple strands of chain hung either from the headdress or around the neck, lying on the back. It comprises bells, nuts, fruits and small vessels of silver, with a central triangular plaque with more little ornaments hanging off that. Together with the large earrings the panoply is a wonderful mixture of Byzantium and the Orient. A large collection of Astypalaian costume is at Liverpool, mainly from Wace's collecting on the island in 1906.

Left A velvet domed cap, the skoufia, decorated with a two-headed eagle and opposed partridges embroidered in metal thread, wire, silk and sequins. Astypalaia, about 1720.

Right A headscarf, chrysomandilo, worked in gold and silver wire at both ends, with a linen reticella edging. The scarf had been given to Queen Victoria and bears her wardrobe label No. 38 in the left corner. Astypalaia, about 1850.

A range of domestic towels were produced in the island. They are narrow plain weave lengths in silk, linen or cotton and sometimes woven with a slight slub. The two ends are worked in a drawn thread technique, and unlike most of the Aegean drawn thread work, which is all white, the embroidery here is carried out in blue and red. The designs are all native versions of those Italian patterns that are found on the blue woven Perugia towels, and must have been derived from them. The towels or napkins are worked in cross and button hole stitch on the drawn thread background. The patterns, usually pairs of animals or birds set on each side of a vase or fountain, are placed in an oblong tablet with a simple border on all four sides. The style and patterns found on these towels are sometimes found on much larger pieces, where they form a narrow border on one side. They are called sheets, but I think that they are covers and are of recent production, copying older pieces.

Karpathos

Karpathos and Kasos were controlled from Rhodes for a short period before they were returned to the Venetien overlords, the Cornari, and remained within Venetian control until given up to the Ottomans in 1537. They were important islands and had much larger populations than Astypalaia or the smaller islands around Kos, but deteriorated as the importance of the crossing between Rhodes and Crete lessened.

The Karpathos poukamiso is the wonder of all Dodecanese costume.

Left and far left The back and front of the Byzantine poukamiso from Karpathos, showing the solid areas of embroidery and how the long skirt is folded to the size required but exhibiting the greatest area of embroidery. This dress was collected by Bent in 1883 and was part of the Helen Stathatos collection. Before 1750.

Right A great poukamiso of Astypalaia, the front worked in the spertonato pattern and the sleeves in a chequered pattern. Before 1750.

The first were collected by Theodore Bent before 1885. He was the first foreigner to show any interest in them and collected nine in all, five from Karpathos and four which were later said to have been from Nisyros, although they could quite easily also have been from Astypalaia. He was told that they had all been last worn over 150 years earlier, which would mean that they were made before 1750. He gave three to the V&A Museum in 1886, and the other two from Karpathos and the three said to be from Nisyros were shown at the BFAC exhibition in 1914 by his widow.

The Karpathos poukamiso is the most heavily decorated of all island dresses, with a feature not seen elsewhere: a method by which a very long dress, the longest is nearly two metres long, can be worn by anyone. A deep tuck is made in the unembroidered part of the skirt, above the deep hem and below the embroidery which is worked all the way around the very deep neck opening. The tuck is folded inwards and can reduce the length of the garment by up to 60 cm if necessary, giving the impression that the poukamiso is being worn on top of a separate skirt. The two Karpathos dresses in the Benaki, and one in Boston, all of them part of the original collection made by Bent, are of silk, whereas all the others are reported to be of either cotton or linen. The weight of the embroidery on a silk ground fabric makes the survival of even three surprising. They all have the same type of embroidery, carried out in untwisted silk using cross and stem stitch, with a plaited braid finishing the bottom hem. Both the front and back of the dress are heavily covered with embroidery in the same pattern, with a different one on the sleeves. They are worked in a laid and couched stitch, using an untwisted floss which is twisted by hand during the embroidery process and then couched, with a different two-strand silk, to make a very tight and firm surface pattern, a difficult and impressive technique which is not found elsewhere.

In four of the Karpathos dresses the pattern is called *spertonato*, which if anything means an expertly made pattern. It is a compressed version of the isolated glastra on the Karpathos valance. The sleeve pattern is a small check in three colours, red, dark blue and dark green, and covers three-quarters of the sleeve. The embroidery is so heavy that the seam

The valance for a bed or bench. The pattern shows a catholic church and a cardinal's beretta with the ribbons, made to celebrate the appointment of a Querini son as a cardinal. Astypalaia, about 1700.

82

at the shoulder that joins the sleeve to the bodice is heavily embroidered over as a reinforcement. The other dresses have a slightly lighter pattern; the border hem and the front carry a narrower block pattern edged with a little worked star, which gives this style its name of *staphylato*, meaning 'with grapes'. The sleeves on this dress are decorated with lines of a small geometric pattern set diagonally.

A number of pairs of sleeves have survived, all using the grape

The front panel of a poukamiso decorated with a copy of an Italian velvet showing an arti-choke or pomegranate within curled leaves. The side border has small plumed birds. Astypalaia, about 1800.

pattern as an edging. The main pattern on these sleeves is a splendid geometric pattern of a square set with rhomboids, to form a design similar to Naxos work. One pair has the field over-embroidered with a small castle in the same range of stitches. The work is so similar to the rest of the work that they must be very nearly contemporary. A wide range of stitches, Roumanian, chain, cross, chevron, Cretan feather and stem stitch in five colours, is used in the embroidery. I take this use of more varied stitches and a wider palette of colours to mean that the work is later, the product of a more mixed culture, showing a stronger influence from the Italians: presumably the Cornaro family that held both Karpathos and Kasos and exposed them to European fashion.

There is no evidence, and certainly no remains, of bed tents. There are valances for free-standing beds and benches and a large variety of cushions. A Karpathos valance which is of particular interest has a main design not unlike a glastra, which is, in fact, a Cardinal's coat of arms showing a church building and at the base the ribbons always shown under a Cardinal's hat. Perhaps this particular pattern was created to honour the three sons of the Cornaro family that were made Cardinals and took up positions in Rome in the seventeenth century.

The square cushions are of two main types. The larger number merely have decoration on one outside edge, so that when the cushions are stuffed and set in tall piles all the embroidered work can be seen.

Part of a bed tent panel with an over-all pattern in two colours of a broad leaf worked in feather stitch and Rhodian cross stitch. Rhodes, about 1700.

84

p.37 The second version has one surface decorated with a pattern that either runs all around the top, leaving a blank centre, or covers the whole of one face. These would have been used spread out on benches or along the bed. The cushions cannot have been used very much; they are objects of decoration and were used for storage as much as display. They would have been filled with textiles that were not in use, or even full of materials such as weaving thread or embroidery silk in store. I have seen them filled with household textile scraps, or even with raw goat hair. The cushions are usually about 40 by 50 cm, although many are very nearly square. The long narrow bolster or pillowcase that is so common in the Cyclades, particularly in Naxos, does not appear to have been made in the Dodecanese.

Above The turnover corners of a large sheet set with blocks of a plant form with birds at the base and in the branches, alternating with a fan-tailed bird or a pot of flowers, each block worked in a single colour. Khalki or Symi, about 1820.

Right A sleeve from a poukamiso, the outer borders worked in Rhodian cross stitch, gobelin, Romanian, chevron and double stem stitches. The central pattern of a squat vase was added later for a richer effect. Karpathos, about 1700.

85

6 The Sporades

The Sporades, the 'strewn out', lie north of Euboea in a line off the mainland at the western end of the Gulf of Volos. The main island, Skyros, is set some distance away from the other three, Skiathos, Skopelos and Alonnisos. They were part of the Byzantine Theme of Thessaly; after the Frankish Conquest they were given to the Venetian Ghisi family, who also owned other islands in the Cyclades. The Ghisi, together with the Sanudi, formed the aristocracy of the western islands, and owned the Sporades until 1390, when they reverted to Byzantine rule. The administration by the Byzantines was so lax, as it indeed was throughout the Aegean, that Venice virtually retained power over the islands until the Ottoman raids into the Aegean, after their conquest of Constantinople in 1453. The islands were conquered again and held for a further hundred years by the Venetians, ruled by an appointed Rector, before finally falling to the Turks in 1538, until they were incorporated into the New Greece in 1832.

Skyros has produced the most engaging and lively embroideries of the whole area: an individual style was created there which carries influences from the Cyclades and Epirus and from an Ottoman tradition as well. The similarities to motifs and figures from the work of Crete derive from the fact that they both stem from similar traditions, rather than that there is a single direct influence from Crete.

p.138, 139

p.108, 109

Fortunately we have Angeliki Hatzimichaili's *Skyros*, in the Greek Folk Craft series of 1925, a detailed and authoritative study of the island which allows one to observe, almost at first hand, the culture and tradition from which these embroideries emerged. Sadly, Skyros, Rhodes and Astypalaia are the only islands where this directed approach was made, and all three proved to be of special interest. I am indebted to Hatzimichaili for her information which I use in this section, and also in the later chapter on techniques where I quote extensively from one of her sources. She describes how the house was organized and gives a vivid picture of life on the island. The one-room house comprised a front living area set around a large fireplace, with its rising conical chimney breast, and a rear part, with a built-in wooden

A ceremonial cushion cover, showing guests carrying candlesticks, ewers and flowers, a mandolin, trays of pastries and rifles carried on the shoulder. They are dressed in Ottoman costume with stocking-net caps and turbans. Four of the smaller figures are dressed in green European dress, wearing European hats. Skyros, about 1700.

partition containing a cooking area and a storeroom, with a narrow staircase leading to a sleeping area.

The front area, *aloni*, is a public area; the sleeping area in the upper part of the partition is the *sofas*, behind a wooden balustrade, *bolmes*, from the Turkish word for a partition, *bölme*. The upper sleeping area has a low railing constructed around one stout, central supporting column, the *stylos*, and both the lower part of the railing and the stylos are elaborately carved and decorated. The bed is usually spread out on the floor of the sofas and consequently there are neither bed curtains nor bed tents, as elsewhere in the Aegean. When not in use the bedding is stored in cupboards set into the walls of the sofas, the *mussandires*, from the Turkish word for a cupboard, *musandira*. It is only in the Aegean that this Turkish-derived word is used; elsewhere in Greece the word used is derived from the Italian *armario*, or from the Persian *dolap*. Clothing was usually kept in large boxes, *pankos* (from the Venetian form *panca* of the Italian *banco*) set against the wall in the living area, or hung on pegs set into the wall in the store room. This short list of derivations demonstrates clearly how the islands have been influenced by both the east and the west.

The main decoration in a Skyran house was the wide range of ceramics and shining kitchen utensils, which were displayed on shelves or hung on wooden stakes fixed into the 'best wall' of the house. The disposition of the furniture dictated what embroidery was made and how it was used. Many of the decorative textiles were woven: the *tavlomantilo* - table cloths and runners - and the *vagioli* - a smaller long cloth decorated with a panel at each end, similar to the embroidered towels. The woven cloths were usually white with a single or two-coloured decoration. Together with the coloured embroideries they introduced a wide range of bright colours into the house; they would be placed on display for festivals and family celebrations, usually hanging on the rail around the sofa, replacing the plain daily cushions.

Hatzimichaili makes the point that I have made elsewhere that for a number of reasons the domestic craft of embroidery was lost, replaced by industrially produced coloured cloths. Fortunately embroidery was revived in Skyros in the 1920s, when girls were taught it in school and so were re-introduced to their local tradition. They used old fabrics when they could so as to produce work similar to the old embroidery, and to reinforce that impression they worked in darning stitch with silk that was obtained by untwisting commonly available industrial multi-ply silk embroidery thread into single strands, to achieve the look of the old untwisted floss silk. This means that most of the embroidery called Skyros is either from the second half of the eighteenth century and the first half of the nineteenth century, or from after 1920.

The embroideries from Skyros divide into three distinct groups. The first comprises small square or rectangular pieces which are cushion covers, short scarves, *tsevredes*, from the Turkish *çevre*, or longer ones, *machramades*, which were used as head bands. The second group is composed of much larger rectangular pieces that might be either

The interior of a house on Skyros. This end of the single-roomed house contains the kitchen and store rooms on the ground floor, through the central door, with stairs leading to the bedroom above. The central column, the bolme, is heavily carved, as is the low railing. Curtains were not permanent but cloths would be hung on the rod as needed. Clothing would hang on wall-pegs and the back wall would be decorated with embroideries and china.

bedspreads or, more likely, ceremonial sheets, *sendonia*, used specifically as sheets for the marriage bed and then used as decorative festive hangings. The third group of embroideries is that used on clothing, mainly for women, but also includes the *tsemberakia*, the small embroidered cloths used for wrapping the heads of babies and very small children, a usual custom in the Near East; the word comes from the Turkish *çember*, a binding or neckerchief.

The cushions and bolsters were used both for the pankos and the small extra bed. They are commonly plain weaves but many celebratory pieces were made for particular occasions - marriages, baptisms, or even perhaps the launching of new vessels or the setting out on a journey. They are made of one width of homespun cotton cut square, 35-50cm.

The design is usually either a large motif placed at each end, or a smaller motif repeated in each corner with small motifs placed between them and a central ornament. They appear to have been worked as a separate face then backed with a stouter, more durable material. The bolster covers are rectangular, worked in repeats of the patterns found on the cushions. Sometimes a floral or leaf pattern on a much larger

A baptismal bolster cover showing men with mandolins wearing turbans and men with candles wearing caps. Skyros, about 1750.

scale is worked into a very stylised oriental arrangement filling the whole surface.

p.100, 105

The longer pieces attributed to Skyros may have been used as sashes, scarves or shawls and are often called towels, following the Turkish fashion. They are always worked on a medium quality fabric. The sashes are about 25-30 cm wide, the scarves and shawls are about 40-50 cm wide and vary in length from 85 to 160 cm. These pieces are always worked on both ends, with the long central portion undecorated, without even a thin border along the sides. The patterns vary from a very Turkish motif repeated exactly on each end to a very informal and joyous arrangment of different motifs worked freely, either in rows or in blocks.

The larger pieces are much more what one expects from Skyran work: decorated in a more inspired way within a native Greek tradition, more spontaneous and lively. A common pattern is parallel rows of different motifs placed at both ends or all over the cloth. The largest motifs are placed at the end of the scarf, and these can be three-masted vessels or large complicated floral sprays repeated twice in a line, and above them rows of humans repeated three or four times, then small single sprays repeated four or more times, with the sequence repeated as required to fill the area. The humans in these versions can be men holding flowers larger than themselves, men in baggy trousers standing under palm trees, and any version of the men found elsewhere in Skyros.

All the pieces are multi-coloured and follow the *grafto* method, by which a design is drawn freehand on the cloth and then embroidered, on one face only, like most Skyran work. The large bolster covers in the Turkish style use a colour range which is brighter and more shiny than the Greek pieces, almost as if they had access to a different quality of embroidery silk. The cloth is either a light woven silk or a silk/cotton mixture, with a few in either linen or cotton. They are all made using a single loom-width of fabric, 40-50 cm wide.

In the second group of embroideries there are two distinct types of sheet, the grander of which has many similarities to an Epirote sheet. The base fabric is very fine linen, with equally fine embroidery displaying a careful and skilled use of the various patterns. The other version is not as fine either in the base fabric - quite often a linen cotton mixture or a plain cotton - or in the embroidery, which is repetitive and a little obvious.

These sendonia are always made of three widths of fine linen or cotton sewn selvedge to selvedge. They were originally embroidered on the two outside panels with a large repeat pattern, usually a floral motif, although some of the oldest sheets have the large cockerel on them. It is unlikely that these were sheets or counterpanes in daily use: if the family bed was on the sofa and out of sight, the cover would never have been seen by outsiders and in a sense have become pointless; they must therefore have some ostentatious, ceremonial use. It is most likely that it is the wedding night sheet common in the

Islamic world from Turkey right through to Central Asia - the sheet that must be shown to have been stained with blood on the wedding night to prove the virginity of the bride, then displayed proudly to the guests. A thrifty society would develop a system by which the same outer embroidered panels could be used again, with a new centre panel for each wedding night. The stained panel would be kept by the wife with her few treasures. As the need for this ritual died the sheets continued to be made, but the embroidery was now placed around all four sides, leaving the centre plain, and would have been used as hangings for festive occasions. Eventually even the centre of old sheets would have been filled in, and this later working can be seen from the change in design and quality of stitching. Pieces that are described as valances are merely one of the side panels which has become separated from the rest of the sheet. The use of a cockerel on these sheets neatly emphasises the occasion by introducing an obvious virile, fertility symbol.

p.129, 130, 132

One is tempted to believe, as with the Epirote embroideries, that the sheets with figures and the fantastic creatures spring from the native Greek tradition, and that the more organised and totally floral sheets are from the equally native, but Turkish-Islamic tradition, that technically forbids the representations of humans and even animals.

p.126

The women's and children's embroidered clothing is more akin to a larger tradition of embroidery found all over Greece and the Aegean shores of Turkey. It is quite fine but does not have the individuality or charm of the other two groups, and will not be treated in great detail here. The *tsemberakia*, the children's head-bands, however, are peculiar to Skyros. The front decorated panel which lies on the forehead is either oblong or half round, occasionally embellished with small coins or tassels. The Faltaits Museum in Skyros has a large collection of these baby head-cloths.

Another group is attributed to Skyros, but they are so similar to Naxos work that even if they were worked in the Sporades, they are merely copies of Naxos work and are considered under that section. A cushion cover from the Fitzwilliam Museum, collected in Skyros by Sir Augustus Daniel before 1910, is a fusion of both styles: a typical Naxos razor-edged leaf motif is set in a trellis, with every cluster of four leaves centred with a fletched cross. The spaces are filled with alternate rows of men dressed in baggy trousers and belted kaftans and a three-branched plant rising out of a stylised two-handled pot. The piece is splattered with a flower shape that may be a pomegranate flower, and a small perky bird - altogether a charming piece. The trellis is a dark green, with a sixth of the trellis having bleached to a gold, although it was green when made. All the men and plant forms are in a soft brown, a gold, pale blue and yellow, with the men's faces, hands and trousers outlined in dark brown.

The repertoire of Sporadic patterns is composed of four main groups: human figures, animals, both naturalistic and fantastic, ships, and vegetal and floral patterns. They can be found on any of the three

A ceremonial bolster cover worked with a Naxian pattern of leaves in a trellis, filled with men dressed in baggy trousers and kaftans and elaborate flower patterns. Pomegranate flowers and birds fill every space. Skyros, about 1750.

Part of an embroidered cover showing a flat stand with an elaborate flower arrangement with naive heraldic beasts opposed and pairs of cockerels set about. Skyros, about 1750.

groups of embroidery, none is used exclusively.

In the first group one finds men wearing baggy trousers, a stocking-net cap that falls over to one side, and occasionally a kaftan-like surcoat with a tied belt. The men brandish swords, carry guns or coffee pots, play musical instruments, hold tall candlesticks or pots with flowers in them, and even carry cockerels. The figures are mainly dressed in a local Turkish-derived style, with one rather grand figure, who would have been a local dignitary under the Ottoman rule, known as the qadi, appearing frequently on the small covers and on the scarf ends. He is usually a central figure, wearing Turkish costume and a Turkish turban instead of the stocking cap. Many of the other male figures must be seen as attendants. Female figures are usually dressed in the local style of a short surcoat over a flared skirt, with a fancy head-dress.

The figurative embroidery of Skyros is quite different to the rest of Aegean Island work; it is exuberant and bold, almost a child's vision of the world. The motifs similar to Epirote work have been simplified and enlarged, so that it is easier and quicker to fill large surfaces with them. A favourite theme which is drawn directly from observation of life is

94

the range of sailing vessels, from a simple rowing boat and a single-masted yacht to the great galleons. One of the most joyous and characteristic examples of these ships is the *goletta*, with sailors strung out along the spars and even standing atop the masts, from which many-coloured flags fly. A seafaring nation understands and revels in the sea, enjoying the vigour and exuberance of the scene, even to showing the shore and the fish that lie just inshore, and even in one showing a mounted horseman on the shore being followed by four of the bizarre animals he is hunting. The joy of these pieces can be seen in the way that the hull is composed of lines of differing bold simple patterns, with the sails worked in contrasting checks of red and white, or of silvered metal and gold silk. This embroidery incorporates a symbol which is quite different to those included in the wedding or church embroideries: it is an icon set in one corner, perhaps a St George with a small dragon, to protect the seamen from the monsters of the deep, a reminder that St George's dragon came out of the sea.

This same joy and exuberance can be seen in the sash border which has the portrayal of the dumpy horseman brandishing two swords above his head, and wearing what appears to be a knitted renaissance costume of doublet and hose, with a cockade in his brimmed hat, rather than the otherwise ubiquitous Turkish dress. He is surrounded by a simple trail of flowers and two knitted blue deer with golden horns. In addition to this European knight Skyran embroidery is full of more local figures of village headmen and qadis, all very forceful, facing forward and wearing impressive turbans, and more often than not surrounded with many attendants. Other pieces show men playing lutes or carrying swords or guns. In one exceptional small square cushion cover, which must be a wedding or christening piece, the pleasure and inspiration of the embroiderer can be clearly seen. In it

A cushion cover with a large flower surrounded by buds and leaves. This form of embroidery is more Ottoman than Greek, and very different to the domestic Sporadic work which is full of humans and humour. Skyros, about 1800.

95

there are thirteen large figures, some carrying large candlesticks, some with rifles or trays of sweets or fruit, and the central figure playing a baglama or lute. These men are surrounded by eight boys who carry the same range of articles, but not the rifles. Most of them are wearing the plebian stocking-net cap, separating the piece from the formal patrician embroideries and revealing it as the domestic celebration it is.

Another side of Skyran embroidery shows two favourite motifs. The first is a human-faced bird, or an animal which is more likely to be a naïve representation of the lion of St Mark, which is still to be seen carved on the walls of houses in Skyros. The second is one particular female figure that is always described as a witch, *xouna*, wearing a long Turkish coat over baggy trousers, with turned-up shoes, and carrying a small flower. They are part of local mythology as magic creatures, and occur often in folk tales and can be seen on pottery and wall paintings.

One of the charming features of these embroideries with human figures is the way in which the figures are drawn in two or even three different scales. A large qadi will be surrounded by small servers; the rigging of the ships will be manned by two sizes of sailors, without regard to either perspective or safety; blank areas of a design will be filled with rows of figures that may be witnesses or spectators to the action, or just filling blank space.

p. 86

p.100

The second group of patterns is of natural and fantastic animals. The most spectacular and attractive of all the natural creatures is the large cockerel. The most powerful of all Skyran images, with its splendid tail that tells of boldness and pride, it stands as a symbol of the character of the Skyran people. It appears in many different forms, and is embroidered on sheets or towels and even on cushion covers and sashes, and in each case is presented boldly, without the flowers and tendrils that encumber most of the other Skyran motifs. It can have a large lyre-like tail or one that bursts into single circular feathers, rather like a peacock, or even a small four-feathered tail. Other birds are parrots, pigeons and doves, the inevitable Byzantine double-headed eagle, and various composed birds that are not meant to be identified.

There are naturalistic horses, invariably mounted by either a qadi or a warrior with swords, but all the other animals are fantastic. A large number of these are hybrid creatures which have been given human faces to increase their strangeness; there are harpies with human arms and legs but with large tails, four-legged, winged and tailed animals with human faces and a shock of straight hair like a nimbus around their heads, *aspithes*, *seirines* and gorgons, mermaids that have female busts but bodies terminating in a leafy tail. Other fantastic animals are lions with long curly tails, four-legged animals with long feathered horns, horned deer, web-footed, mouse-headed deer, and rampant heraldic lions and birds.

The main wealth of Skyros came from its seafaring tradition and it is appropriate that sailing vessels should be featured proudly in their embroideries. The main vessel is the fully sailed three-master, the goletta. It appears on one piece with a classical prow and a large human

figure at the stern, with little sailors disposed about the rigging. The rest of the embroidery is filled with figures and birds, isolated flowers and stars, the sea is filled with fishes and horsemen ride on the near shore.

Other boats are the small two-masted sailing ships with one bank of oars, *trechandiria*. Embroiderers also talk of a number of other vessels on embroidery, such as the *bratseres*, *tachyplia* and *kernitsia*, but I have not been able to identify them. There are a few scarfs with buildings on them, mostly church buildings and monasteries, and they must be mainly cloths for baptisms. One of them shows the parents and the god-father, *koumbaros*, from the Italian *compadre*. After being used for the ceremony these cloths are usually donated to the church for use in later services.

The textiles with boats on them have recently been copied very extensively, but with simplified designs. It is quite easy to identify a twentieth-century piece by of the poverty of the drawing and the simplicity of the execution, even if it is worked on a piece of old fabric.

The last group of Sporadic patterns is composed of those pieces with floral and vegetal designs, which are the commonest. The basic form of the floral embroidery is a repeated motif of one or more units, freely drawn and loosely scattered. These floral patterns are very Turkish in style, and the way they are used and placed on the fabric is very similar to the great embroidered and printed cloths made in Istanbul, and also to the *peskir* and *pestemal* that were made all over the western seaboard of Turkey. The single unit is usually a central vase or leaf or even a bare stem, out of which rise a number of curling branches which themselves shoot into flowers or large leaves, and further branches with smaller flowers and leaves. Each complete motif is contained in itself and perfectly designed to be used as a block repeat. The same motifs can be

found in many of the textiles from other islands that are close to Turkey, but also in textiles from Trikeri on the Greek mainland. The similarity to the Trikeri fabrics is explained by the fact that that part of the mainland near Skiathos had been populated by inhabitants from the Sporades who were fleeing from the pirates that infested the area in 1800, taking their repertoire of island patterns and designs with them.

The basic flower motif is called *lales*, from the Turkish word *lale*, for a tulip, and the version with a tendril and leaf curling over the top is called *kampouraki* from the Turkish word for a hunchback, *kambur*. These names emphasise the influence that Ottoman embroidery has had on the development of the tradition in Skyros. It is as strong as that in Epirus and certainly stronger than in the rest of the southern Aegean. The floral motifs are sometimes embellished with little mannikins or fantastic birds and animals.

How this small island developed such a diverse tradition, and from where it derived its motifs has been the subject of much speculation. The human figures look most like figures from Byzantine, Egyptian Graeco-Roman and Coptic textiles influenced by Byzantium; the horse and riders look like many of the representations of St George and St Minas, and the little mannikins are like the endless little figures in the Coptic tapestry weaves from Egypt. The animals also look like those in the same tapestries, particularly the deer and long-eared rabbits. The fantastic animals come from the Frankish tradition and are very similar to misrepresentations of real animals in the bestiaries and pattern books from Europe, which were well known in the Aegean. The ships and buildings are those found on ceramics in Turkey and the Dodecanese.

The large sheets with the broad borders filled with many isolated different motifs are very similar to the sheets from Epirus. They employ the same techniques and many of the same patterns, such as the extraordinary three-towered building, and the way that the flowers and pots are placed in the corners of the plain centre. I think that the Skyros cloths are part of the same tradition as the Epirote, and not necessarily copies. There are so few of the Skyros pieces that it is conceivable that they were made by journeymen embroiderers who came from Epirus. They may have been imported from Epirus, where the proof of manufacture is greater, but no firm case can yet be made for that. The quality of the great Epirote sheets and the Skyran pieces with the large cockerels suggests professional rather than domestic production, the domestic origin of the smaller pieces is undoubted.

The embroideries are all worked on one face in single-strand untwisted silk in bright but fugitive colours, with some groups of embroideries using a different range and quality of thread. Skyros had a great tradition of domestic silk dyeing, which may account for the wide range of colours used, but also perhaps for the colours having faded and changed so much. The later pieces have stronger, more enduring colours, which is not necessarily to their advantage. It is mainly in the embroidery for clothing that one finds the use of gilt metal wrapped onto a silk or cotton core, or even a metal strip which is used without a needle to create the embroidery. This is mainly used for the bodice embroideries and the tsemberakia.

Men's costume is rarely decorated, other than a little sober braiding added to the waistcoat. The main women's costume, the poukamiso, is of the European cut, with a full skirt gathered onto the bodice, which has a deep cut neckline and full sleeves. A short jacket called a *gouna*, with or without sleeves, is worn on top of the bodice in such a way that the embroidered ends of the sleeves are shown to full advantage.

The special feature of the Skyran poukamiso is that it is made of two materials: the bodice is a finely woven silk and is dyed a dark red, blue or green; the skirt is always white and of cotton or linen, and sometimes a mixture of either with unbleached silk as the weft. The bodice is embroidered around the neck and down the extended neck opening, usually with a pattern of a small repeated flower set in a line hanging from a base, although it can be much more elaborate, forming a single or double wreath, and exceptionally, like the Bosanquet piece in Newcastle, embroidered with the large-tailed bird, which is such a feature of larger embroideries. The main embroidery is at the base of the sleeve, and is usually a repeated block of a floral or leaf pattern which is derived from Ottoman embroidery, and can be seen on Istanbul, particularly Tepebashi work, and on Bursa work.

p.79 The embroidery is carried out in gold or silver-wrap silk thread, almost certainly an imported product. The sleeve is further decorated with applied gold or silver braid, ribbon, or embroidered bands of a small geometric pattern, placed below the embroidery and sometimes along the sleeve joint which runs along the top of the arm. It is even used as an insertion braid to join the two sides of the sleeve. The end of the sleeve is finished with a sewn-on band of complicated bobbin lace, copying punto in aria, bebilla work or even a length of crochet lace. The whole bodice, with its gold embroidery, is so bright that the costume itself is called 'the Golden'.

The skirt is of linen or cotton, composed of four widths, which are left unjoined at the bottom for about 15 cm. The base of the skirt is called the *skouta*, and the embroidery of the skouta consists of isolated floral and leaf patterns in a large range of coloured silks. The edge of the skirt is finished with a narrow band of a small repeat pattern, which is taken up the sides of the unsewn ends of the skirt panels. The costume is finished with a poukamiso of coloured material worn over the white poukamiso, but shorter, so as to allow the embroidery on the bottom poukamiso to show. This overskirt is not embroidered but of a highly coloured weave or print. The women's costume is completed with a number of the scarves and cloths already described.

The range of stitches is large. The bodice is embroidered with a range of flat stitches suitable to the wrapped metallic thread: darning, basket and a squared couched stitch. The skirt is embroidered with cross stitch, stem stitch, a form of feather stitch which is called corn stitch, and satin stitch. The same range, single and double darning, and occasionally chain stitch, is also found on the other domestic embroideries.

7   *The Northern Islands*

Chios and Mytiline, also called Lesbos, Icaria, Lemnos, Samothrace and Thasos lie in the northern Aegean between Greece and the Turkish coast. They were part of the Byzantine Empire and after 1204 were given to various families of the Italian Republics that were establishing commercial trading empires in the east. They then passed to the Ottoman Empire, and eventually became part of Greece. Some other islands in the north Aegean are Turkish.

The largest of these islands is Chios, which has been researched historically and ethnographically in a number of volumes by Dr Philip Argenti. He includes embroidery in his book *The Folklore of Chios* (1949), and although he states, quite correctly, that there is nothing of particular interest about its costume or the embroidery, mentioning that they follow the fashion of Europe, he nevertheless published a large volume on the costumes of Chios in 1953. This volume deals extensively with the banal costume of the islands, referring to and illustrating at length a few undistinguished pieces, thus emphasising the poverty of the embroidery tradition in the island.

The Genoese made Chios their centre in the Aegean, and from it they administered their commercial enterprises throughout the region and also gave help to the independent Genoese pirates that operated in the eastern Mediterranean. The island was made into a Limited Share Company, called The Mahona, controlled by the Gustiniani family that represented other mercantile families of Genoa. The Mahona introduced into Chios many crafts from Italy and Europe and can be said to have established the first industrialised society in the Near East, with a large number of textile and leather manufacturing units. A system of duties to be paid on both imports and exports was then established which provided most of the revenue for the company.

Members of the Genoese Silk Mercers' Guild, the 'Arte Serica', brought to Chios new techniques of silk weaving, particularly velvet, and by 1480 a well developed industry had been established. Very soon manufacture and trading replaced agriculture. It is estimated that about a fifth of the island's labour force was involved in the silk industry; and

A scarf, tsevre, with a row of three-masted vessels with sailors in the rigging and, unusally, two very realistic horses, a row of a wedding couple and a newly-planted tree, seven rows of the 'hunchback flower' and, finally, a row of the pattern called 'the princess on the galleon'. Samos or Mytiline, about 1750.

industrial cloth production grew so fast that Chios was no longer able to supply sufficient local raw materials to feed it, and by as early as 1354 raw materials, particularly silk, were imported from the rest of the archipelago, Anatolia, mainland Greece and even from the Caucasus. This continued well after the Genoese left in 1566. This early industrialisation contributed to the destruction of a domestic embroidery tradition at a period when it had newly started to flourish elsewhere in the Aegean. Lord Charlemont mentions in his *Travels to Chios* in 1749 that: 'the principal and lucrative trade is in silk, of which not less than 30,000 lbs is annually produced, and by far the greater part of it is manufactured into velvets, damask and other rich stuffs, mixed with gold and silver.'

Chios was the entrepôt for much of the trade between western Europe and the Ottoman Empire; English, Dutch and French trade vessels all made a stop at Chios before going on up to Pera or to Crete on the return journey.

Argenti mentions that four types of embroidery persisted in the island: *tripito*, cut work, *azour*, drawn thread work, *kasinaki*, filling stitch, and *stavrovelonia*, cross stitch work. He makes particular reference to a group of embroideries called *kalimeres*, meaning 'good days', which are small embroidered squares which would be hung in a room, bearing a

A cover worked on cotton. The centre is the windmill pattern with the vanes open and shut, with an interrupted border of square motifs. Chios, about 1800.

A breast cloth, stithopano, worked on fine cotton. A motif of four squares within a twelve-pointed medallion is placed centre and in each corner, with six repeats of a floral spray filling the ground. The whole cloth and each square motif is outlined in a narrow border of needle-weaving in cream silk. Chios, about 1820.

legend such as 'Good Morning' or 'The Lord is our Help'. I consider these message samplers to be more the product of the Victorian Age than the Greek islands. The ones that I have seen are of a particularly trite sentiment, with an equivalent poverty of embroidery technique. Printed cotton squares were imported from the Turkish mainland from about 1750, and worn by women as scarves, aprons and breast cloths. They were called *kallimkeries*, which is a dialect form of *kalimkar*, the Persian and later Turkish name for these printed squares, and derived from the Persian word for 'pen work'. Gradually the imported term changed into the Greek word *kalimeres*, with its meaning of 'good day', and a product was created to satisfy the new meaning of the word.

The older tradition of small embroidered squares is the *stithopano*, breast cloth, used to cover the opening left by the very decolté bodice of the Chian poukamiso. They are pieces of silk or silk and cotton mixtures about 35cm square, embroidered in cross, satin and split stitch in a machine twisted polychrome silk and occasionally a metal strip. These squares were used also as handkerchiefs, particularly as the fashion of the low-cut bodice died out. The Chian poukamiso, which is of the oriental cut, and the short jacket worn over the poukamiso, are occasionally embroidered with bands of geometric patterns of no very great interest. They are either white or monochrome, and I have

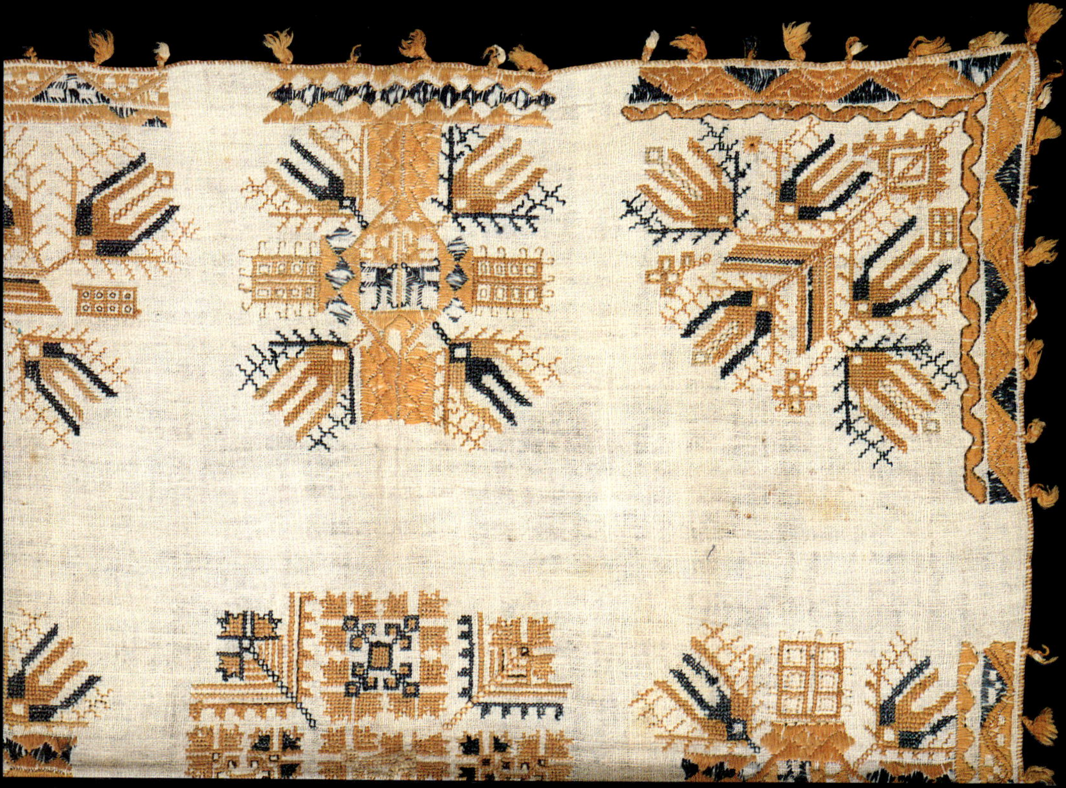

seen no pieces that might be from before 1900. The bridal costume from Kalamoti in Chios at the Benaki Museum is uniquely gaudy and surprising, quite unlike anything else in the Aegean.

The remnants of domestic household embroideries are very few: there are some square cushion covers in various museums but no large curtains or sheets. The cushion covers are always embroidered on linen in a darning stitch which attempts to look like a jijim weave. They are exactly like the *yastik* that one finds all over Aegean Turkey, and even the patterns are more reminiscent of Turkish weaves than of Greek embroideries.

The other islands do not appear to have a strong tradition of embroidery with separately distinguishable characteristics. The pieces attributed to them are all late pieces much nearer in style to coastal Turkish work rather than to Greek island work. Thasos has some cushion covers that are very similar to Naxian work, usually on a coarse thick cotton weave with dull embroidery; the patterns are over-all, geometric and usually monochrome.

Mytiline is mainly represented by scarfs made of a fine Turkish silk or silk/cotton mixture, embroidered at both ends with small isolated motifs. Wace has distinguished them by saying that they all have end warp fringes tied with tassels of pink and green silk, but that feature is also found on many pieces made in Anatolia. There is a certain amount of white work which is attributed to this island, but again it is of a common type that could have been made in any town in the whole area.

Facing page, above A cover worked with an interrupted border. Each corner contains a five-flower motif, the sides have a version of the windmill pattern and in the centre five square motifs form a cross with corner flowers. Chios, about 1820. *Far left* A sampler for curtains worked on linen in a basic Naxian style, with trial patterns worked in the border. Thasos, about 1800. *Left* Part of a cover in darning stitch, with an ancient pattern found in wall paintings set within an outline trellis of stars and hexagons. Thasos, about 1800.

Right The end of a sheet decorated with partridges and stylized tulips and hyacinyths worked in couched stitch. Samos, about 1800.

8 Crete

The history of Crete in the Middle Ages and the Renaissance is inextricably tied to Venice; after the Fourth Crusade Crete was allocated to Boniface of MontFerrat, together with large areas of northern Greece, because he was one of the prime movers in the attack on Constantinople. Soon afterwards, presumably when Venice had realised that owning the Aegean without Crete was a mistake, he was persuaded by the Serene Republic to sell the island to them for 1000 silver marks and for other property in mainland Greece, including Epirus, from which he could obtain an annual income. Venice then took from 1204 to 1212 to wrest Crete from the Genoese who had, even earlier, established themselves there.

Once the Venetians controlled Crete they colonized it for the next forty years with groups of military and commercial immigrants. These new immigrants, unlike the Franks elsewhere in the new Frankish Greece, ousted the local landowners and formed separate, isolated communities on their acquired land. The Venetians were not absorbed into the community; they maintained their close links with Venice, established the Latin Church and started negotiating with Mamluk Egypt and Saracen Syria for trade and mutual military support. Their attitude to the local population was quite different to the new chivalry in Greece and the other islands, and engendered a spirit of revolution against the invaders that has become a feature of the Cretan character.

Crete, as the Duchy of Candia, was from 1206 until 1669 the flower of the Venetian Empire in the east, and it was not until 1645, when the Ottoman Turks started to attack the island with considerable force, that the long-established treaties and agreements began to deteriorate. Venetian Crete had always impeded Turkish progress into the Mediterranean, and although it had held out against the Turkish attacks, and had even survived the Siege of Candia which lasted twenty-two years, the Venetians finally relinquished the island to the Turks in 1669. The full history of the Venetians in Crete has never been written, and the rows upon rows of original documents on Candia remain undisturbed in the Venetian National Archive.

A detail from another portion of the skirt border illustrated on page 113, showing both main motifs. One is a large urn set about with flowers and fruit, its stand flanked by two doves. Above the vase two men ride long sea monsters with golden tongues, with a simplified gorgon holding her double tail set between them. At the base a woman in European dress is opposed by a Cretan man, in his baggy trousers, playing a violin. The second motif, of a candelabrum, has two dragons at its base. Before 1720.

The Turks had a very troublesome occupancy of Crete for over two hundred years, before they were finally driven out in 1897. From then until 1913 Crete was an autonomous island, with Prince George of Greece as High Commissioner. After the Balkan Wars it was, together with the northern Aegean Islands and Macedonia, incorporated into Greece. By then the island had been greatly impoverished by the continual insurrections of the Greek population against the Turks: the first in 1841, followed by that of 1858 and the last, most disastrous rising, of 1866. Reverend Henry Fanshawe Tozer, travelling in Crete in 1880, describes the results of that last rising, showing how Crete had suffered in its attempts to gain freedom: 'Every village that we passed through, and all that we could see along the hill-sides, had been plundered, gutted, and burnt; nothing but ruins met the eye; it was as if a horde of Tartars had swept over the face of the country.'

The main influences on Cretan folk art, including embroidery, are principally Venetian and Italian, and later Ottoman. There is little evidence of Hellenistic influence in any of the art, although the repertoire of designs includes many features that are usually described as Byzantine. These entered the repertoire of Cretan art motifs through the omnipresent Greek Orthodox Church, which persisted and flourished throughout both Venetian and Turkish occupations, producing the finest of all Greek icon painting.

The costume of Crete had been commented on by travellers from the fourteenth century, mostly disparagingly. They commented on the oddness of the dress, its shape and particularly the low-cut neck opening, but none of these descriptions leads one to expect the beauty and invention of the embroidered skirts. The embroideries of Crete present one with a particular problem, in that because they are immediately recognisable - invariably skirt borders with polychrome Italianate patterns, mostly in Cretan feather stitch - one assumes that

A skirt border decorated with two repeated motifs, a double-headed eagle set above a round vase terminating in three carnations, and a gorgon holding her double tail above a column and flower sprays. Every space is filled with pairs of strange birds and flowers, as is the border. Detail shown as the frontispiece. Crete, about 1750.

108

they have been closely studied and that everything would already be known about them. This is quite wrong; they have in fact been little studied and present both the collector and the student with a series of unanswered questions.

The embroideries were first collected by the British Consul at Chania, Thomas B. Sandwith, during his stay there from 1870 to 1885. His daughter, Charlotte Boys-Smith, comments that he bought the embroideries to help the poor and that he was not interested in collecting. In one of her letters she writes: 'When my father bought these petticoats, etc, the peasants still wore them, I believe, on Fete days. But their extreme poverty after the frequent disturbances in the island, obliged them to part with them, and they often wept as they brought them for sale.'

Thomas Sandwith gave the largest part of his collection to the South Kensington Museum in 1876, and his grand-daughter, Priscilla, donated a further part of the family collection to the History Museum in Crete in 1977. The Sandwith Collection in the Victoria and Albert consists of the 160 pieces given in 1876, and further pieces given by his grand-daughter in 1953 and 1967. There are 56 skirt pieces, some complete skirts and one or two panels from different skirts, 104 bobbin lace lengths called *aratzidelles*, and two complete *colletti*. The collection of Cretan textiles was added to by various donations and finally augmented by pieces from the Dawkins Bequest. This is the largest collection of Cretan skirts anywhere, thanks mainly to Sandwith's collecting. When his collection was put on show in 1876, by the South Kensington Museum, as it was then called, the reviewer comments, 'Mr Sandwith has bought up nearly all that was to be found in the island.'

The embroideries of Crete can be divided into two main groups: those from the Greek tradition, which are the skirts, cushion covers and

Detail from a Cretan skirt border with some motifs derived from Italian renaissance art: a double-tailed gorgon, hares and naive lions, and others from Byzantium: the crowned two-headed eagle, leaves turning into fishes and harpies. Compare to the illustration on page 170. Crete, about 1650.

a rare curtain, and those from the Ottoman tradition, which are the chemise borders, women's trousers, belts and scarves. Additionally, there are a few pieces derived from Italian fashion of the seventeenth century, mainly the short cape called *colletto*. During the late nineteenth century, when the Arts and Crafts embroiderers in Europe discovered the folk embroideries of the Balkans and Central Europe, there was very great interest in Cretan work, and a number of small ateliers set up in Crete to produce new pieces, many using the unembroidered portion of old skirts or filling in the blank spaces on existing embroideries.

Ecclesiastical embroidery for both the Latin and the Greek churches was made in every century. Many were within the classical traditions and therefore not especially identifiable as Cretan work, but there are many examples of domestic embroideries being re-cycled to make copes, vestments and altar furnishings.

The best of surviving pieces are the skirt borders. They come from the long shift-like poukamiso, which did not have a bodice but hung from two shoulder straps supporting a thick gathered band that would have sat on the breasts. In some adapted skirts, and possibly in later versions, the gathered high waist and shoulder straps are replaced by a simpler gathering and a sleeveless bodice with a wide neck opening, more like a Turkish chemise, the *gömlek*. Each skirt is made of five loom widths, 50 cm wide, of a fairly heavy, coarse home-woven linen, neither flared nor tapered. The only decoration is placed around the bottom of the skirt - in early skirts it is about 25 cm deep and in later ones it can be as much as 70 cm. These skirts are the only embroideries that bear a date and occasionally even a name. The earliest known is dated 1697,

Above A skirt border with a double-headed eagle with its breast converted to a heraldic shield set in a wrought-iron pattern, with gorgons set between each repeat. Again pairs of birds and floral motifs fill every space, including the base border. Crete, about 1750.

Right A skirt border made at the end of the period of their production. Every motif has been simplified, the wrought-iron pattern has been shattered, the birds and sea monsters are barely recognisable. Even the gorgon in the base border has become a stick figure. The silks are all imported and industrially dyed. Crete, about 1850.

two years before the Turkish conquest, and other dates are 1733, 1757 and 1762. Some small pieces, cushion covers, have inscriptions which are quite illegible.

There are four types of embroidered decorations on the skirts. Three are Italianate patterns that one would expect, the fourth is a repeat geometric pattern very similar in style to Cycladic work.

Of the three Italianate patterns, I consider the earliest to be a narrow frieze, 25-30 cm, composed of container and flower motifs from the universal Mediterranean repertoire of patterns in late medieval and renaissance times. These motifs stand on a narrow border lined top and bottom and usually filled with a flowing tendril and flower strip. The motifs above the band are usually two alternating self-contained designs, and the way they lie suggests punto in aria lace, a strong indication that that is where the motifs originated. This earliest version is usually in monochrome silk, red or blue and sometimes, more rarely, in bi-colour, red and green, red and blue and, most rarely, red and black. The monochrome version sometimes departs from strictly floral motifs by introducing opposed birds, and in one spectacular skirt collected by Sandwith the floral motifs are set above a frieze of men and women dancing among stylised flower sprays. The figures are dressed in renaissance costume, the men wearing a variety of hats and caps and even crowns, and the women in the basic poukamiso with narrow sleeves.

The second Italianate version is the most commonly found. It is worked in polychrome silk using up to seven different colours, in feather stitch, stem, satin and chain stitch and small knots. The pattern is still an open-topped frieze set on a band but has now broadened to

70 cm. The decoration in this version is extremely varied; the basic
motifs are still floral and vegetal but they have become very lavish,
usually with sprays rising from a container or a trellis of leaves, all filled
with figures, birds and animals, sometimes naturalistic but also with a
large repertory of fantastic creations.

Two common motifs are the gorgon and the double-headed eagle.
The gorgon is woman above the waist and a two-tailed fish below,
usually with human arms and hands that each hold one of the two tails,
a design certainly derived from sixteenth century Italian pattern books
for lace and cut work. The double-headed eagle is a Byzantine state
motif, symbolising the position of Byzantium looking both east and
west - the Christian counterpart of the Janus head. In later
iconography, particularly in the Christian parts of the Ottoman
Empire, it became both a religious and a political symbol; Skanderbeg
used it as a symbol of Albanian resistance against the Turks in the
sixteenth century, and in Epirus it became the emblem of the
endurance of the Orthodox Church. Other animal motifs are the pairs
of opposed birds, dogs, fishes, fish-tailed dragons, snakes, rabbits and
human-headed frogs which are used to fill any space within the
complicated design. They are used with great invention; the figures are
usually independent but sometimes formed out of the lines of the
embroidered pattern.

The human figures placed in these friezes are often pairs of a woman
in a long skirt and a man playing a fiddle, *lyra*, sometimes placed within
a roundel, and they are, of course, referred to as either the engaged
couple or, in a more romantic western terminology, the 'Idyll'. In
addition to these realistic figures there is a large repertoire of surrealistic
human figures, such as human-headed harpies, little mannikins, imps
and the upper halves of gorgons, which are used perched on tendrils
and flowers, very like the grotesques and putti of renaissance
embroidery in Italy and northern Europe. The repertory of motifs is

Above A wedding cushion cover,
the centre medallion containing
a gorgon with a double tail
which has been converted here
into the Virgin Mary as Regina
Coeli, the tail becoming the blue
cloak of the sky. Crete, about
1800.

Right A skirt border of five different vertical designs each composed of many motifs of fruit,
flowers, pairs of humans, animals,
birds and mythical beasts. The
main elements are double-
headed eagles, an aproned lady, a
large vase with sea monsters (see
detail on page 106). The whole
decoration is set above a narrow
border of heraldic emblems,
crests, birds and a little chequered
man in a leafy wreath. Before
1720.

more akin to Skyros and Epirus than to other islands in the Aegean, where there was practically no development at all of human or mythological figures in the tradition.

The third version of the Italianate style has a broad central panel about 30 cm deep contained within a continuous frame, flanked top and bottom by a row of scallops with an inset motif, or a row of isolated motifs again set top and bottom. The main border can either be a squared-up version of an Italianate skirt design or a flowing curled tendril and leaf pattern. The motifs are the same as for the previous type, worked in polychrome silk, and the Cretan feather stitch has been augmented with herringbone, satin, stem and split stitches.

Sandwith's daughter comments in one of her letters that she thought that the Italianate skirts all came from the Sphakian district, and that while other districts had regional costumes of their own, they had little or no embroidery. No other region of Crete has produced such a distinctive series of embroideries, so perhaps one must accept her comment and not attempt to place the embroideries anywhere else.

p.43

The fourth version is quite different. It is based on a geometric pattern which can be seen in an early pattern book, *Essempio di Recammi* by Tagliente, published in Venice in 1524. The geometric pattern is usually set in blocks of 3½ rows within a border, top and bottom, which contains one row of the pattern. The top band is sometimes surmounted with a row of a tree pattern, or even, as in an example collected by Sandwith, a row of birds viewed sideways, with an outline extended wing, reminiscent of the Azemmour bird, itself a development of a Mamluk design, yet another example of this influence in the Aegean. This bird, in a slightly different drawing, appears again in Cretan geometric embroidery, set into a long panel that might be either skirt widths or even aprons. A panel, described as an apron, shown in the Burlington Fine Arts Club (BFAC) Exhibition, has two panels of these birds set into a design of Naxian leaves, and is

tentatively attributed to Ios,on the basis that the characteristics of the piece place it between Crete and Naxos, and Ios has this position geographically.

A large range of stitches is used in the skirts. At first appearance it seems that the Italianate ones are worked in feather stitch alone but, in fact, these other stitches are used, as they are in all the other skirts: herringbone, satin, stem, split stick, chain stitch, running and double running, eyelet and French knot. The monochrome borders are in feather with an outlining stem stitch, and the geometric skirts are worked in long-armed cross stitch, double running and double darning.

The quality of the work varies considerably, both in the drawing of the pattern and the execution of the stitches. One is inclined to say that earlier versions are better made than later ones, and that the original inspiration of the drawing is preferable to the later one. This is particularly true of the copies that were made later, which I call 'revival' pieces.

The same Italianate style is used for cushion covers, which are usually rectangular, 1½ times as long as broad, worked on a linen cotton mixture in polychrome silks. The design is a broad border on all four sides containing the flowing tendril and leaf pattern, and sometimes including a bird. In the centre there is a roundel containing a motif of either a petalled rosette, a sunburst, a double-headed eagle, a gorgon or an engaged couple. The space between the central roundel and the borders is filled with flower sprays in the corners and small flowers elsewhere. A cover in the V&A Musuem is filled with three rows of roundels, some half roundels, and filled with flower shapes and one two-headed eagle and, exceptionally, has no outer border band.

Some short lengths of embroidery are almost certainly from larger pieces worked over-all. Sadly no piece has survived large enough to

A ceremonial cushion cover, un-usually in a monochrome red silk worked in feather stitch. The central medallion has four pairs of birds set about plant forms, which are repeated in each corner. The border is filled with an Italian renaissance motif. Crete, about 1800.

114

allow us to speculate on the original usage; there is no tradition of bed curtains, so they might have been hangings used for some other decorative purpose. They have mainly survived because they were of the size that allowed them to be converted easily into ecclesiastical textiles, mainly copes. As the Catholic Church was diffused throughout Crete there must have been a very large use of vestments and church decorations, but perhaps they were all made in the Latin style and were never distinctively Cretan. The occasional Greek-style piece must have been for the Greek ritual.

Crete had a substantial Moslem population even during the Venetian occupation, and was naturally influenced by its Ottoman neighbours. There were Moslem quarters in all the main towns, as there were Jewish ones, but they had always been smaller than the native Greek population. However, after the Turkish conquest in 1669 the number of Moslem inhabitants grew, so that by the time of the Greek War of Independence in 1821 there were only 130,000 Greeks to 160,000 Moslems, including the Janissary Corps that had recruited a large number of Greek-speaking Cretans. It is therefore not surprising that there should be a parallel Ottoman tradition alongside the native Greek one. These Cretan Ottoman embroideries follow the mainland Turkish tradition so closely that it is extremely difficult to be dogmatic about what is Turkish and what Cretan, a problem already encountered in the embroideries in Skyros.

Apart from the expected squares, *cevre*, and sashes, there are loosely woven linen poukamisos, with standard Turkish embroidery in polychrome silk and metal-wrapped thread, made in five loom widths, copying the conventional skirt. Also a range of women's trousers which are embroidered on the leg, around the band at the calf and on both outside faces of the trouser legs in staggered rows of floral sprays, reminiscent of the Persian *nakhse*, worked in chain, stem and satin stitches.

A textile collected by Sandwith has a conventional Turkish pattern of a curved branch with leaves, which has been later converted into a small church cloth by the addition of an embroidered gate placed in the centre. It is clearly a church gate surmounted by a cross, and in the open leaf of the door there is a mitred priest dressed in what appears to be Latin rather than Orthodox vestments - a splendid example of the way in which traditions fuse and in which national origins become submerged.

The costume of the Latin population was that of continental Italy, but the native population, both Greek and Moslem, wore local dress. The men still wore baggy trousers, a shirt and waistcoat, as the women continued to wear the poukamiso and the small jacket. The poukamiso was adapted to the full renaissance style and it is this skirt that was heavily embroidered. The small light collar cape, the *colletto*, was also taken up. It must have been introduced by about 1650 and survived well into the 1800s. It is composed of a light Turkish linen weave with inserts of bobbin lace, called *aratzidelles*, a local dialect version of

115

reticella. The strips are all locally made, mainly coarse bobbin lace and some crochet. The V&A Museum Sandwith collection has over a hundred of these strips and two complete *colletti*.

The accepted theory is that standard Greek Cretan embroidery died out about 1800. All the visitors to the island remark that although the traditional costume is worn occasionally it is no longer made, and that girls wear their mothers' costume that they themselves can no longer make. When Louisa Pesel was Directress of the Royal Hellenic Schools of Needlework and Lace in Athens, from 1903 to 1907, she was instrumental in reintroducing the teaching of embroidery into the state school system. In so doing she also revived the patterns that had died out in the islands, and introduced into the repertoire patterns taken from classical decoration. In an article for *The Burlington Magazine* on

Cretan embroidery, written while she was still in Athens, she mentions the reproductions that were made in the school copying the old skirts, using Morris silks that were untwisted and reduced to the thickness of the original silk used, and which could be mistaken by 'the unwary amateur' as the older work. The base linen was similar to the earlier fabric: often plain lengths of the old material were cut from original garments and embroidered. After 1913, when the state educational system was introduced into Crete, there was a revival of the folk patterns, both as new pieces and as over-embroidery in the new style on old pieces. I have seen Turkish, Bulgarian and European embroideries so over-worked.

It is interesting to see in this revival work the introduction of a number of new motifs - St George on horseback and his dragon, a many-legged spider, and a new version of a monster. These revival pieces are more often worked on an undyed grey linen in Cretan feather stitch and six or seven other stitches in a silk which fades, which warns Miss Pesel's unwary amateur that it is a recent piece. The colour range is rather dull and has faded so badly that it is difficult to see how they ever deceived. Revival pieces were not only made in Crete: the sudden publicity that they received from the exhibition at the South Kensington Museum, and their inclusion in the stitch books by Pesel and various publications by *The Studio*, meant that Cretan patterns appeared in many table cloths and hangings worked by Victorian amateurs.

Above A Cretan bolster with an illegible inscription. Rescued from a destroyed church in Chania in 1887, where it had been used as an altar fitting. Before 1750.

Left A revivalist cover aping the older work. New motifs, such as a horned devil on an elephant and spiders, join older bird and floral forms. Crete, about 1900.

9 *The Ionian Islands*

The Ionian Islands have had a very long association with Venice, whose interests in the Adriatic and Ionian Seas started in the middle of the eleventh century. Corfu was one of the main stages on its trade route to the east, even during the Neapolitan Angevin occupation in the thirteenth and fourteenth centuries. This commercial interest became a political reality in1386, when the Venetians finally occupied Corfu; they held it for over four hundred years, defending it against a series of attacks by the Ottomans. After the disastrous Turkish raid of 1537 they repopulated the island with immigrants from Italy, and from the established Venetian outposts in Epirus and the other Ionian Islands.

It is therefore not surprising that Ionian work shows more of the European than the Aegean tradition, which was open to many more different influences. Ottoman influence is very light: they never ruled the islands and did not affect the style of the domestic crafts. Certain pieces have been attributed to specific islands, particularly to Corfu and Levkas, mainly because they were bought or found there; it is very difficult unarguably to assign any one embroidery to a specific island. It would, however, be reasonable to argue that those embroideries with Turkish motifs are more likely to be Epirote than Ionian, and Epirote in this context includes the Venetian outposts on the mainland.

In 1864 the Ionian Islands were ceded to Greece by Great Britain, and from that time their particular identity was lost. The references to Ionian embroidery as a distinct tradition are all after this date. There are no collections in Venice of Ionian work, which would, after all, be seen by them as a provincial, if not colonial, version of original work. Once again it is Dawkins and Wace who started collecting in the islands in about 1906; there is a particularly touching comment in one of Dawkin's inventories of about 1910, where he says of a collection of sheet border fragments that he had bought: 'all these came from Cephalonia, having been got there by 'Old Orient' man in raiding the monasteries, etc, of the island.' Old Orient was one of the few shops that sold Greek folk art in Athens, mainly textiles, and the comment brings home how the islands were slowly denuded of their

A bolster cover showing a winged angel with the head of a Byzantine empress, flanked by a kaftanned attendant leading a horned beast. The background is filled with humans, heraldic beasts and floral motifs, and the ends have a row of the horned beasts alternating with simplified flowers. Split, stem and cross stitch worked on a drawn thread ground. Levkas, before 1750.

119

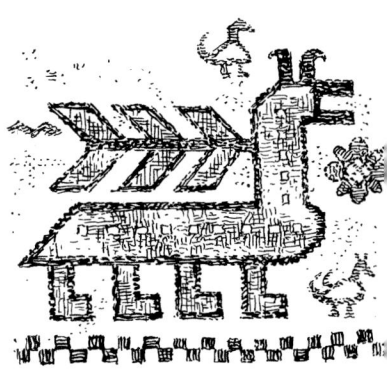

embroideries, to be sold in Athens to new collectors, who were in very large part foreigners. Wace comments that many of the pieces bought at that time had 'clearly been used in a Church, as was shown by the wax with which they were plentifully bespattered.'

The main population lived in town houses during the long Venetian occupation, and followed styles that developed in Italy. Both the French and British influenced it further during their brief protectorates of the islands, when the multi-storied terraced house was introduced. It is this harmony of styles that today gives the capital its pleasing architectural character. The country houses were either farmhouses consisting of two rooms, one for the family and the other for animals and farm implements, or they were terraced houses copying the urban style. Both were fairly rudimentary, undecorated and very simply furnished.

In urban houses the bed was a fixed feature, in the Italian manner. It was made up as a renaissance bed with sheets and blankets covered with a spread. Cushions and bolsters were placed on the bed, and the whole assembly was apparently covered with an embroidered cloth called a *bakaleto*. The literature indicates that girls spent part of their time in preparing the bed furnishings for their dowry. Sadly I have never seen anything that is specifically called a bakaleto, although from the form of the word it should be a cloth used to keep the bed tidy. In the rural house the bed was a trestle set on boxes which were used for storage; it was usually set in a corner, covered with the bedding and a number of cushions and bolsters. There are no references to bed curtains, and no embroideries have been found that would be used as curtains.

Henry Jervis mentions in his *History of Corfu* (1852): 'One circumstance, however, attracts the attention of strangers, and that is the size and beauty of their beds, this peculiarity arises from their not being seizable for debt; much money and care is, therefore, usually spent upon the adornment of the bed.... In former days, the working of the bed-linen occupied the young women's time till their marriage; and consequently was profusely ornamented with a coarse description of lace, very much resembling old point lace.'

I shall discuss these embroideries in four groups: drawn thread work, solid ground work, large sheets or covers and decorations on garments.

Drawn thread work is invariably worked on linen, with every other thread, both warp and weft, being withdrawn, a preparatory process leaving an open net onto which the embroidery is worked. The ground cloth is therefore very loose and distorts easily, so it is always worked on a fixed tambour frame, with a solid border anchored to the frame. The threads are not withdrawn on the whole surface of the piece to be worked, but patches of the original weave are left. These areas are held in with a whipped stitch and the enclosed area of the solid fabric is then embroidered with stitches different to those used for the drawn thread area.

The stitches used are those dictated by the drawn thread ground – cross stitch, tent or whipping stitch and satin stitch. The embroidery is in polychrome twisted silk, although white silk and linen thread are also used. When metal thread is used, it is invariably copper or nickel-plated, silver or gold, wound on a silk base and worked in a tight chain stitch. Solid metallic wire, *sirma*, is also used in the same way.

In addition to drawn thread work there are a few pieces where that technique is combined with pulled thread work. This is the technique where the fabric has been loosened by the removal of some of the warp and weft threads, the remaining threads then being pulled together with an overcast stitch, creating holes in the ground fabric. This is then either over-embroidered, or the overcast stitching which pulls the threads together is worked in coloured threads, making a decorative effect by itself.

The patterns found in drawn thread work are either geometric or animal-based. Most geometric work is found in the bolster and cushion covers; these are usually worked on a single width of a fairly fine linen, 45-50 cm wide. The bolster is usually three times as long as it is wide, whereas the cushions are square or sometimes 10-15 cm longer than wide. They are worked in polychrome twisted silks, predominantly red, blue and green, with subsidiary colours such as yellow, brown and white. The ground infill made of the tent or whipped stitching is usually white or blue, which has now become a pale green. Unlike any

A cushion cover with a central octagon, surrounded by two octagons containing eagles, four medallions with smaller eagles, and a field full of small motifs. The border is of geometric and floral forms with triangular corner decorations. Worked in split stitch on a drawn thread ground. Ionian, before 1750.

other Greek island work the blue in Ionian work is made from woad, which was grown in the islands, not an imported indigo, which may account for its tendency to oxidise to a green.

The patterns used are composites formed of a number of regular shapes, the most usual of which is a star or a square set diagonally on one point in the middle, with corners filled with quarters of the central shape. The bolster repeats this format three times to fill the whole oblong, with the intervening space filled with scattered geometric patterns, including geometric versions of the fat bird, and small stylized human beings. Occasionally, instead of a central star there is a central octagon or medallion surrounded by other octagons and the usual geometric shapes. The whole ensemble is clearly inspired by woven textiles, brocades or velvets, taking up the oriental influence found in so many Venetian textiles of the sixteenth and seventeenth centuries.

The cushions with octagons are very similar to a traditional Italian design; the two cushions in the Musée des Tissus in Lyon are the finest of this version, and have a double-headed eagle embroidered in most of the small octagons.

The bolsters and cushions with animal shapes, and even the occasional human, are more numerous than the others, and have been collected with greater enthusiasm. The animals are those of the renaissance Italian repertoire and can be seen in Italian embroideries from the fifteenth and sixteenth centuries. The most common of the animals is a deer. Its heavy horns lie straight back from the head, with as many as eight pairs of tines. The deer comes in two versions, the large one has a solid monochrome body usually in-filled with a number of smaller animals and birds in a contrasting colour, thus avoiding what was clearly unacceptable to the embroiderer - an area of

Part of a bolster cover with three large deer surrounded with heraldic lions, birds and stylized Byzantine eagles. The ground is full of deer and birds worked in white. Worked in cross and split stitch on a drawn thread ground. Ionian, before 1750.

unadorned colour. The smaller one is a subsidiary pattern, with the body filled with small square blocks. The other most common animals are a curvilinear lion, a two-headed eagle and many different versions of the ubiquitous fat bird. The design follows that of the geometric type: a single motif for the square cushion, repeated three times for the oblong bolster.

The solid ground work is within a native Greek tradition. It is invariably on a fine linen and carried out in either cross stitch or a very finely executed split stitch, using rather dull polychrome silks. The colours are red, blue, green, yellow and black, with blue and red predominating. The shapes and sizes for both cushions and bolsters are the same as those for the drawn thread work.

The patterns on the solid ground cushions are mainly a widely spaced four-armed branching pattern spreading out from a small central geometric motif, with the ground filled with sparsely drawn vegetal and geometric motifs. The geometric patterns are much later than most other Ionian work, and have become simplified versions of the motifs, reduced to the simplest way of executing them in cross stitch. In style they are more like the borders found on the tunic dresses and some of the simpler sheet ends, which are all late work.

The solid ground bolsters are usually filled with repeat animal patterns, mainly the antlered deer and the bird. The motifs are set out in staggered horizontal lines, sometimes quite irregularly and, more often than not, drawn in a very naive manner reducing the shapes to a conventional form. The stitch is primarily an even-armed cross stitch, but double running or a small gobelin stitch is used for the straight lines. These animal patterns appear to be found only on bolsters.

Ionian embroidered bed sheets are different to those of Epirus or the Aegean; they follow a more conventional tradition, clearly made for continuous use rather than exclusively for celebrations. Like all sheets of this period, they are made of five strips of linen, about 40 cm wide, hand or machine woven, sewn selvedge to selvedge with the seams lying across the bed, making the sheet 200 cm wide and about 270 cm long. One side has the decorated border about 25 cm deep running all along its length and down two strip ends at the sheet ends. Very few complete sheets are found in collections; usually only the two end strips have been preserved. The decoration is usually worked in a twisted silk in cross stitch which can be either open-spaced or worked continuously in both directions. The colours are those traditional in Ionian work - red, blue, green, black and a cream or yellow – but it can be drawn thread needle work, cut work and broderie anglaise, and wide flounces of lace are often added.

The patterns are all very similar: a limited number of motifs arranged into larger block patterns. The standard is a block of two opposed peacocks on each side of a fountain or a vase, alternating with another which can be either a cypress tree or a branch decorated with flowers and leaves. The Ionian peacock is related to the Epirote bird, but where that is curvilinear and freely drawn the Ionian bird is stiff and angular,

as is inevitable when it is worked by counting threads for cross stitch work. The blocks are liberally filled in with smaller birds, the long-antlered deer and simplified versions of the double-headed eagle. In many cases the pattern is merely a collection of random motifs not even tied together with a wandering branch or tendril. There is a narrow border on the outer side only, always a version of the wreath or tendril pattern, contained within two bands of square chequers, often with the end warps twisted along the outer edges to make a simple fringe.

When sheets are not decorated with the peacocks they have other blocks of trees and branches, again filled out with all the same subsidiary motifs, including opposed pairs of a bird more elegant than the fat peacock.

Although the embroidered sheet tradition is an old one, I believe that the majority of the pieces found in museums today are mostly late eighteenth and nineteenth century versions of the older sheets.

The standard Ionian dress is a long poukamiso of a heavy hand-woven linen gathered into a high-waisted wide band below a short bodice. Square sleeves are attached to the bodice with insertions of bobbin lace or of needlepoint bands. The sleeves are formed of two straight widths of a finer linen, which often has two or three warp stripes of an ecru silk along both selvedges. The neck of the bodice is deep cut and embroidered on both sides; the neck opening, *trachilia*, is fine white work, based on a whipped open hole and stem stitch, edged with a narrow band of needlepoint work. Other versions of the neck opening embroidery are carried out in chain stitch with areas of satin and stem stitch.

The sleeves are embroidered along the lower edge with a narrow band of cross stitch, seldom more than 7 cm deep, in a simplified version of the blocks used on the sheets, either geometric or incorporating reduced versions of the various birds and animals. The skirt has a narrow band of embroidery at the base, seldom more than 8 cm deep, very like the sleeve embroidery but simpler. Again the small blocks of pattern are repeated, usually two or three worked in sequence.

Borders for covers, each showing opposed birds and animals around a floral form set above a border with a repeat pattern. Worked in cross and stem stitch. Ionian, about 1800.

10 Epirus

Embroideries from Epirus have usually been studied as part of the island tradition, although geographically they should be treated as Greek mainland work. However, stylistically they are so different to the neighbouring provinces of Macedonia and Thessaly, which are part of a larger Balkan tradition of costume and embroidery, that it is right that they should be discussed here.

Epirus was the largest textile centre in the Balkans and produced a great deal of commercial embroidery on an industrial scale, providing most of the Balkans and many parts of the Ottoman Empire with court dress and uniforms. This aspect of Epirote embroidery needs to be studied separately and is not covered in this book. The other embroideries, both professional and domestic, which have many similarities to Aegean work, are studied here as part of the same tradition.

When Epirote embroideries first came to the attention of collectors, the dealers tended to call the whole group after the capital, Yanina, under a variety of spellings - perhaps as a balance to the practice of calling all Dodecanese embroidery Rhodian. Sometimes pieces from Istanbul and Skyros that had a similar appearance were identified as Yanina, even, as Louisa Pesel commented in her *Burlington Magazine* article of 1907, some pieces that we now know to be suzani, from Central Asia. The similarities in stitching technique, style and the repertoire of patterns would excuse some confusion in a few pieces, but the embroideries of the Sporades and the Istanbul atelier pieces are distinctly different and should be easily distinguished from Epirote work.

Once one has accepted a general attribution to Epirus, it is necessary to classify the large body of work into subdivisions, permitting a detailed system of study and identification to be developed. It is now quite impossible to allocate each sub-group to a particular production centre with absolute certainty, despite the information collected by Greek scholars since the initial naming by the dealers. The information, sadly, has gone; it was already too late even at the beginning of this

The corner of a large cover, the main border consisting of attendants in Ottoman dress carrying the Sandjak flag alternating with large floral motifs and occasional green parrots and red deer. Large ewers with bunches of carnations are placed in the corners of the main field. Epirus, about 1720.

century to collect the basic information directly, so one must now rely on such evidence as the pieces themselves present.

At the piecemeal division and allocation of Greece to various Frankish families in 1204, Epirus was part of the area given to Boniface of MontFerrat. In 1214 Michael Angelos, who was a cousin of the Emperor Isaac the Second and had been appointed as one of Boniface's lieutenants, left Boniface's side and set himself up as Despot of Epirus, ruling the province, including what is today south Albania and the northernmost of the Ionian Islands – Corfu, Paxos and Levkas. In justification he stated that he was only inheriting the Byzantine province from the Governor of Arta, who was his father-in-law. He re-established in the province an outpost of the remnants of Byzantium, where the Hellenistic culture of Byzantium could survive. The Despot united the mixture of races that lived in Epirus at that time, which had always been a problem to the Emperors in Byzantium; he also managed to remain independent of both Byzantium and the Venetians and Franks who had taken the rest of Greece.

Epirus was finally conquered, with most of the southern Balkans, by the Ottomans at the end of the fifteenth century. Together with a portion of present day Albania, it was incorporated as one of the Sandjaks, ruled by a junior Bey reporting directly to Istanbul. Epirus became the frontier at which the Ottomans met Europe, represented by the Venetians who held the Ionian Islands and the fortified towns of Parga and Preveza on the coast of Epirus, and Valona and Butrinto on the coast of Albania.

An important date in Epirote history is 1788, when Ali Pasha of Tepeleni became governor. He gradually turned Epirus into an independent state, virtually ignoring the Sultan in Istanbul. He waged war against the French who, under the Treaty of Campo Formio in 1797, had gained control of the Ionian Islands from Venice which had previously held them for over 400 years. Ali Pasha used the period of both the French democracy and the Septinsular State, 1799-1807, to consolidate Epirus on the mainland, to regain Parga and the other coastal towns and to turn Yanina from a small provincial capital into the cultural and industrial centre of the Balkans.

There is no evidence that irrevocably establishes that all one type of embroidery was worked in Epirus and another in the Ionian Islands or in the Venetian outposts on the Greek mainland. However, accepting that Yanina was the textile centre of the Ottoman Empire in Europe, and that it provided the whole of the Balkans with their elaborate embroidered uniforms on an industrial scale, it is certain that an equally strong tradition of both professional and domestic embroidery also existed. It is reasonable to identify certain embroideries as being part of a Greek, Turkish or Latin tradition, but ideas were interchanged and professional work was made for all three markets. The majority of the surviving embroideries must date from the eighteenth century, with very few surviving from earlier times.

Yanina influenced fashion throughout the Balkans, as is evident from

Four decorated borders of a large sheet resewn into a large cover, the two short sides together forming the right-hand panel. The pattern is a branch with eight hyacinths and leaves. These sheets were used again and again with new centres and were stored in this form. Epirus, about 1750.

Albanian, Bosnian, Bulgarian and Hungarian work. It was itself influenced by the Ottoman court and by Europe, through Venice, and set out to make textiles for all of them. Not only were finished articles exported but many Epirote journeymen or refugee tailors travelled in the Balkans and the Aegean, producing Epirote work.

The industrial production of textiles and garments in Epirus was in the hands of three craft groups, the *derzidhes*, the *sirmakezi* and the *kazzazidhes*. The *derzidhes*, from the Persian, *derzi*, were the tailors, the *sirmakezi*, from the Turkish word *sirma* for metallic thread and metallic lace, were the workers in metal thread, and the *kazzazidhes*, from the Turkish word *kazzaz*, a silk manufacturer, were the workers in silk, mainly embroiderers but also the makers of braid.

Epirote embroideries are here sub-divided into five groups – Yanina, the spotted group, celebratory, coastal work and a domestic group.

The first group has most commonly been called Yanina for the longest time. Its principal distinguishing features are the exclusive use of floral motifs and the predominance of herringbone stitch. Herringbone is the stitch that is called 'oriental' by Pesel and 'feather' by others; running chain and stem stitches are also used for outlines and borders. The patterns are composed of flowers and leaf shapes, the two most distinctive ones are an elongated, slightly curled leaf laid bending alternately right and left, the other is composed of blocks of conventional serrated leaves and multi-petalled flowers, attached in sixes or eights to a bent stalk. The designs would have been rather freely drawn directly onto the ground fabric, making for rather erratic repeats. Motifs are taken from Ottoman textiles, both woven brocades and embroidered quilt covers.

Yanina work is mostly found as bed sets, composed of bolster covers, small pillow covers and sheets, although very few complete sets have survived. The sheets are the wedding sheets described in the section on Skyros. Few complete original sheets have survived. The tradition was that the borders were fitted to a blank centre which, once used, would have been taken out and preserved. The borders were sewn together to make a large square and stored, to be used again for another wedding. This has happened to the pieces in Washington and to the two in the Benaki Musuem. One composite piece in the Benaki uses a three-petalled conventional tulip with a three-sectioned leaf, and another copies an Istanbul quilt cover of a flower set within two hyacinths. Pieces in other museums have often been treated in the same way.

The sheets, including the embroidered portion, are usually about 200 cm long by 170 cm wide, and made of joined strips of a fine linen. The design is carried out in silk, usually dark blue and green, with the petals of the flowers in a brick red with highlights of cream and a strong golden yellow. The fact that a light, fine linen was used clearly indicates that the sheets were not expected to be used daily as a regular domestic textile.

Long rectangular bolster covers were used on a sofa as well as a bed. They were made in pairs, of one width of fine linen, usually just under

p.92

Three borders of a large sheet resewn into a cover of three panels. The design is a large pomegranate or artichoke set within two curved sprigs of carnations and leaves. Epirus, about 1800.

131

50 cm wide and about 120-150 cm long. Each face was sewn to a
coarse linen back, from which most have now become detached, and
are now often found sewn back to back. The embroidery is set in a
broad band on all four sides, leaving a long rectangular blank centre
into which large bunches of leaves and stylised flowers are set in all the
four corners.

The spotted group has, of course, an abundance of monochrome
spots introduced into any large area, but there are usually small square
spots left void, allowing the white base cloth to show through, although
sometimes they are worked in a different colour, or a much smaller
coloured dot is placed within the small unworked area. Although these
spots add to the decorative appearance, technically they allow large
blocks of long darning stitch to be broken into shorter stitch lengths,
making for a more stable surface. This spotting technique also occurs in
most of the other groups. These pieces are worked in lustrous
polychrome silk in darning and double darning stitch, on a fine loosely
woven linen, with back stitch to outline and fill. A small tight chain
stitch is also occasionally used. Sometimes the darning stitch is laid so
that it looks like split stitch, although I do not think that that could
have been the intention, as split stitch does not fit in with the general
appearance sought.

These pieces are quite early and have been extensively recycled for
other uses, and can be found in many different forms. The most
spectacular of them is the bible cover made of a cushion cover showing
St George on his horse, at present in the Monastery of St Stephan in
the Meteora.

The whole repertoire of Ottoman motifs used in contemporary damasks, velvets and embroideries are found here in this group, together with western ones derived from Italy and Venice. The eastern motifs are tulips and carnations, leaves, ewers and birds, a harpy wearing a crown with a peacock's body and tail but booted human feet, a large-tailed peacock and a hook-beaked bird, always identified as a parrot, which in Indian and Persian literature carries messages between separated lovers. The western patterns are the lions, snakes, horses, horsemen and humans. Some of these are clearly locals dressed in native costume, with an occasional bizarre European headdress. This would support the theory that Christian ateliers worked alongside the Moslem ones, catering for a different market or, what is more likely, the restriction against portraying living beings was less strongly followed in new, multi-racial Yanina.

The spotted bed covers range between 160-250 cm by 200-270 cm, made of four loom widths sewn together vertically, with the embroidered portion integral to the cover. The quilt covers, which may also have been used as decorative panels in a European context, range between 122-165 cm by 200-270 cm and are usually only three loom-widths wide. Bed covers are decorated in a broad band on all four sides, with a large isolated motif set in the inner corner of the blank centre, while quilt covers are worked over-all, the ground full of a repeat pattern contained within a narrow border.

The broad band is composed of a main border about 40 cm deep, with an outer narrow border of 2 cm contained within an embroidered line. The main border usually has a repeated sequence of two or three motifs, which can be tulips of various forms, ewers, tall cypresses and pairs of opposed peacocks set about a tiered fountain or a ewer full of flowers, and a large tulip alternating with a curled artichoke leaf. Rarer motifs are perfume phials, small buildings, mythical beasts and human figures. One shows an attendant at a wedding playing a lyra. The narrow border is invariably a continuous ribbon of leaves and flowers set on each side of a tendril. The borders are encrusted with hundreds of small parrot-like birds filling every empty space; they climb up the vertical features of the main borders, run along the top of the border and are set around the four corner decorations of the otherwise blank centre. The corner ornaments are usually not found in the border.

A few borders have survived which are unique, non-standard patterns. One at the Benaki Museum has a naive design called 'Aesop's Fables', showing a number of mythical animals: a lion with a woman's head and all four feet and tail ending in heads with open mouths, and a winged snake with a host of other fantastic details - forms that one sees in the altar cloths described later. The piece shows signs of considerable over-embroidery; certainly the main outer border is by a different hand and done at a later date.

These embroideries were extremely valuable articles, used only for special occasions, and would have been kept folded and stored and consequently they retain the brilliance of their original colours,

p.141

A wedding bolster cover, showing the bride and groom on either side of a ewer, themselves flanked by the companions. Parrots, eagles, dogs and flowers fill the background. Epirus, about 1750.

p.18

p.126

making one doubt their age. Many must have been made in the early eighteenth century and some even earlier.

The celebratory textiles, mainly marriage and betrothal pillows and wedding bolsters, invariably portray humans, which makes them the most touching and most desirable, as far as collectors are concerned, of all Epirote work. They would have formed part of every girl's dowry, worked in expectation of what was to be the greatest day of her life, when she would leave her father's house to be led away by her husband's friends to be installed in his house. She worked onto the bolsters and cushions portraits of herself and her groom-to-be, supported by the *koumbaros*, the best man, flanked by relatives on horseback, attendants and grooms carrying rifles or candles or musical instruments. These pieces also bear all the marriage symbols: a water ewer as a symbol of purity, the bride is described as 'chaste as cold water', an abundance of flowers - tulips, hyacinths, carnations and stylised roses - and a whole menagerie of animals for good luck - fat partridges and parrots, dogs, cats, leopards and even women-faced harpies, hardly an emblem of good luck, but perhaps they are there to avert bad luck. I know of only ten wedding bolsters, but I hope that there are more elsewhere to be discovered.

There are also wedding cushion covers; versions found are the bride on a horse being led to her husband, bride and groom standing on each side of a ewer, she holding the large ewer and he a small cup to accept the water, a symbol of her surrender, a horseman surrounded by four attendants, the bride flanked by two figures mounted on bizarre horses, and another where two *palikars* are set on each side of an enormous ewer and flowers, with small grooms placed oddly in the composition.

135

This pattern is also worked as a border on nuptial sheets, with the wedding group placed in the centre of the one side, flanked by two groups of opposed peacocks set on each side of a ewer sprouting a large bunch of flowers. There are two versions of this wedding sheet in Burton Yost Berry's collection in Chicago. The first is remarkable, as the bride and her father are not the traditional local figures but are dressed as Europeans, most probably Venetians; she wears a floppy velvet cap set inside a tiara, with a ruff around her neck, the man wears a high-crowned hat with a brim in four points, making the costume late sixteenth-century Venetian. A sheet in Edinburgh has the characters in the standard costume of the rich in the Ottoman Empire.

p.153

Another pattern has young soldiers or court officials on it, and has survived as a complete cover. It has a main border 25 cm deep of a repeat of two red-cheeked youths, wearing kaftans and a small mob cap, set on each side of a bouquet surmounted by a large three-petalled tulip, with a tall green cypress separating the repeats. In a fragment in Washington the figures have acquired a tress of black hair and stand around a two-handled vase of carnations and thin tulips. In both cases the figures carry small flags, which may identify them as attendants to the Bey. The whole embroidered area is filled with parrots, long-eared four-footed animals, and various flowers.

p.126

A dramatic motif found in Skyros pieces as well - a castle with three crenellated towers, two of which imprison a figure with upstretched arms - occurs in a number of pieces. The emblem of the castle is much more in keeping with Dodecanese work, where it copies a motif found in late Byzantine icons, but here I think it is a reminder of the episode when the Grand Master of the Knights of St John, Ferdinand d'Hérédia, was given rights to the Venetian base at Vonitza, from which he was to attack and take Epirus from the Byzantine despots. The attack was launched in 1378, the Knights were defeated by the forces led by the Lord of Arta and d'Hérédia was captured and held between 1378 and 1381 for a ransom of 8,000 florins. If this speculation is correct then it is a powerful proof of the persistence of a motif copied from piece to piece long after the original inspiration.

p.139

Another historical design portrays a white-faced king wearing a European three-pointed crown, doublet and hose, mounted on a caparisoned horse. This alone of all Greek embroideries carries a memory of the Frankish occupation which lasted nearly five hundred years. The design is a common renaissance pattern, the rider and hawk, found in silks and embroideries from Italy and Spain and in a Venetian Epirote piece discussed later. In this piece the blocks of single darning stitch in one colour are not broken up by spots, but by a small diagonal diaper very like the weave on Perugia towels. There are two versions of this pattern, the first was collected by Wace and Dawkins in Epirus in 1901 and divided between them; since then portions of it have been given to the V&A Museum and others are still owned by Wace's family. The other version was found in Greece later, and was part of the Stathatos collection given to the Benaki Museum. In this piece, the

p.51

basic form of the horsemen is retained but the shape has been simplified and is less diapered, and the horsemen are placed between very oriental motifs of tulips, hyacinths and perfume phials with insets of winged birds. The earlier version places the horsemen between candelabra, which break into monster animal heads with red tongues, like Italian work of the early sixteenth century.

This group is worked on a fine linen in lustrous polychrome silks. The borders have usually been detached from their unembroidered centres and preserved as strips.

Part of a border to a cover, showing mounted knights on each side of monster-headed figures. These are Frankish Lords, with white faces, wearing European crowns and armour, with the horses caparisoned in a western style: memories of the Frankish occupation of the thirteenth century. Another piece of this cover is in the Victoria & Albert Museum (T.431–1950) and a similar piece is in the Benaki Museum (11222). Epirus, about 1750.

The fourth group, 'coastal' work, includes the corpus of work which was made for use by the Latin communities, mainly for Catholic churches, of which there was a very large number in the Venetian-controlled coastal towns. These pieces would either have been commissioned by the church or made to order by members of the congregation and then offered to the church. They are often family pieces originally made for some domestic ceremony, and therefore often have no specific church emblem such as a cross worked into them. Among them are altar frontals and communion rail cloths, curtains, lectern cloths, humeral veils and towels placed below icons for them to be wiped after being kissed.

The altar frontals and communion rail cloths are long, narrow pieces, copying those found in northern Italy at the same period. In the Orthodox Church altars are covered completely with a cloth, the *endyti*, which is never embroidered, so they must be for the Latin Church. The pairs of curtains are those used in front of the sanctuary gate, similar to the doors in an orthodox ikonostasis; the other, shorter pieces may be lectern cloths or humeral veils.

The Roman Catholics took over the Orthodox churches for their

services and only built their own churches later, doing exactly what the Muslim Turks did when they conquered new lands. The towns were Parga, Preveza and Arta, on or near the coast of Epirus, and Butrinto and Valona in Albania, all administered from Corfu. Parga was Venetian from the thirteenth century until 1819, when it was sold to Ali Pasha of Yanina. The fleeing Christians took with them everything they valued and placed them for safe-keeping in the churches in Corfu and Levkas.

This group was associated with Parga by early collectors. The majority of the pieces were bought, not surprisingly, in Corfu and Levkas, and were identified as local work. It is probable that they were made by professional ateliers in the fortified coastal towns, which had very large mixed populations of Catholic Italians, Greeks and Albanians. They show a very strong Italian influence in the repertoire of motifs, in technique and in usage; one must escape from the idea that it was only in Yanina that embroideries were made, even if a great deal was produced there.

These pieces are worked on the finest linen, usually two loom widths joined vertically to make the wide, long cloths, or single loom widths for the veils. The long cloths must be altar frontals or rail cloths: they are the wrong shape for sheet ends or quilt covers, and they make no sense as domestic curtains. They have a deep panel of decoration, composed of a band 12-20 cm deep, which runs all along the bottom of the piece and rises upwards at intervals into the body of the textile for about 60 cm, forming five compartments which are filled with a series of repeated or different motifs. The top third of the cloth is left blank, which would allow a lace superfrontal to hang there.

A number of these pieces have survived, two complete ones in the Royal Scottish Museum and fragments of others in a number of museums and collections. The two complete long panels in Edinburgh are, in my opinion, the best of all Epirote work. Both panels were clearly made for the same purpose and must be atelier work. Both are decorated for three quarters of the total width, worked in darning stitch in lustrous untwisted silk, in blue, red, green and white. The first panel, 230 x 91 cm, is divided into five compartments, in each of which

A panel, either an altar frontal or a communion rail cloth, divided into five compartments, four with a winged angel surrounded with flowers, castles, birds and animals, each block separated by a repeated column of three motifs. The border is a frieze of castles, mythical beasts, humans, birds and flower forms. Epirus, coastal work, about 1750.

there is a repeat of an angel figure, indicating a church usage. The angel has a small square green face from which a red feathered head ornament arises; on each side of the small face there are two white roundels which, in a different drawing of the head, could be either eyes or cheeks. He has green wings with straight green and red feathers and wears a red bodice on which a pair of braces appear to be drawn. Below the bodice there is a blue skirt decorated with a small curvilinear bird. Each representation of the angel is separated by a broad vertical border composed of three blocks of floral patterns. The bottom-most of these is a roundel topped with a small half figure, the middle block is three Turkish tulips and the topmost is a floral version of a round peacock tail mounted by a pair of affronted birds.

The wonder of this panel is the border that now runs along the bottom edge, although originally it may have run around three sides. It is a frieze composed of naively drawn motifs, which are almost an identifying feature of this work. The motifs are as follows: a three-towered castle with the four upper windows each framing a figure, a pair of opposed birds, two different floral blocks, two affronted lions with long arched tails which frame a block composed of four women standing around a fountain, a mounted horseman, a repeat of a floral block, a prancing lion, a lady in a wide skirt with long Turkish sleeves, the mounted horseman again, the four ladies and the fountain, two birds facing a vase with a carnation, two affronted lions, but without the long tails this time, set on each side of a repeat of the four ladies around the fountain, and finally a galleon with sailors standing in the masting and framed in the hull.

The angel in this piece is very similar to that in the panel worked on a drawn thread base which is identified as coming from Levkas. This piece also has a number of the bizarre motifs found in these ecclesiastical textiles. It is clearly part of the same coastal tradition and may have been part of a church textile or even of an alb.

The second altar frontal, 225 x 91 cm, reverses the format of the previous piece. This time each of the five compartments carries a block of different embroidery and it is the main outer border that is worked with a repeated motif. The five blocks are, reading left to right: a central

The five compartments of this panel each contain a different collection of motifs. The separating columns also contain different motifs but the bottom border repeats two motifs, a pair of mounted men carrying a flag standard and two floral compositions. Epirus, coastal work, about 1750.

139

vase with flowers rising from it, flanked on each side by a lady and a man and a ewer topped by two horsemen and their two attendants; then a floral motif composed of a large tulip, two trees and a large roundel; the next one is a mounted horseman, flanked by five attendants, surmounted by two vases and a large vessel with rowers; the next comprises two ladies dressed in the local custom, standing on each side of a vase of flowers, with a large castle at the top with prisoners in the towers and soldiers between the towers, the castle is flanked by two peacocks. The final block has a large tulip framed in a garland of leaves, surmounted by two large harpies. The background is filled with small birds, flowers and vases. The vertical columns separating each of the panels are of three types, each composed of blocks of different motifs: one has an eagle, a double branch bearing flowers, an antlered deer and a geometric branch, another has an antlered deer with two different vase patterns, one above and one below, and the last column is formed of two large hooped leaves filled with flowers separated by a small floral block. The whole panel is bordered at the bottom by a continuous frieze of alternate blocks of two opposed horsemen on each side of a cypress tree, and a small floral block. There are no specific religious emblems on this piece.

Panels separated from a third hanging are divided between three museums, the Benaki, St Louis, and Edinburgh. The piece when complete must have had five panels, edged on three sides by a narrow border of a vine tendril entwining a carnation, a rose and a sprig of leaves. Inside this outer guard border there is a wider border on the long side which acts as a frieze to the panel above it, composed of blocks of different isolated patterns separated by columns or short cypress trees. The whole panel is further divided vertically by generous broad strips which are of two patterns. One is composed of two alternating floral blocks based on a crude vase and branch, and the other of a random column of flowers and small animals and birds. The centre of the panels is filled with a haphazard collection of vases with flowers, eccentric double-headed eagles with very feathery wings, strutting birds, sailing vessels with oars and cargos of birds, and filled with little human figures and birds. The whole piece is so eccentric that

Above Two compartments from a church cloth, similar to the illustrations on pages 138 and 139. Each block has a collection of different motifs, and the border has a repeat of peacocks and ewers and three men and poplars. Epirus, about 1750.

Right A large cover with a main border of a large tulip set within two hyacinth sprigs alternating with a perfume vial set within two poplars, above a narrow border of a continuous meander of flowers and leaves. Green parrots run along the top of the border and red ones line the poplars. A ewer with a bunch of carnations is set in each corner of the main field. Epirus, about 1700.

140

it must be an individual creation similar to the two previous pieces, and part of that Epirote tradition most allied to a Venetian one.

A fragment in the Benaki may be part of another frontal with different patterns. In this panel the border is composed of alternate repeats of two floral blocks, and the vertical column dividing the panels is a repeat of a block of roses, tulips and hyacinth flowers set on a network of stalks. This border is very similar to those on domestic epitaphion cloths made for the Orthodox church. Only one panel remains, and is filled over-all with a pattern of a winged eagle alternating in rows with small double-lobed six-petalled roses, leaving a great deal of the field fairly open.

The splendid naive motifs in the borders of both pieces, and some in the panels, are not unlike the carvings on the wooden doors of churches in the Balkans, particularly those at the Templar Church of St

Nicholas in Ochrid and at the convents of Rila, Vidine and Sleptcha. They are also found on the wooden ikonostases of St Panteleimon in Nerezi and of St Stephen in Kastoria. Many can also be seen in the stone carvings at Prespa.

A pair of curtains from these church embroideries has survived. They would have been used in the ikonostasis hanging between the pillars of the ciborium at the Royal Door. One leaf is in the V&A Museum, the other in a private collection. Each leaf is 249 x 96 cm, and composed of two lengths of fine linen sewn vertically. The decoration on each leaf is composed of a field divided into seventy-five squares set in fifteen rows of five, surrounded on three sides by a border. The squares are filled alternately with large features and with smaller framed motifs. The large features are of four types of bird, three versions of mounted horsemen, one of which is apparently riding a large hare, two men standing by a fountain, which is repeated once, and another of two men standing by a tree, a lion and three blocks of a floral pattern. The small motifs are birds, long-eared four-footed creatures, a man with raised arms, and sprays of flowers.

The border of these curtains is of two separate patterns; if hung together the inside and lower border of each curtain is a thick spotted tendril which is interrupted to allow alternate three-petalled tulips and roses to sprout from it. These borders have been worked at the same time as the curtain, and when hung originally, the outer edge would have been hidden behind the jamb of the reredos door and would, therefore, have been left blank. When the curtain was moved it was found necessary to complete the third side. This was embroidered with a thicker twisted tendril, again spotted but uninterrupted, from which sprout a three-petalled tulip and a sectioned pomegranate. Although using the same darning stitch, this border is clearly drawn differently and worked by a different hand, presumably later. The fourth, upper edge has no border.

A number of other shorter pieces were also made as part of the same group. They are long cloths made of one width of the same linen, and use the same repertoire of patterns. They are embroidered in the same silk and mainly use the same stitches, although one piece, a humeral veil, is worked in a four-sided stitch. They are neither towels nor scarfs; if they are part of the church textiles then they would be lectern cloths, icon aprons or even humeral veils. The decoration is at both ends and clearly is to be seen hanging down. Some are decorated with a narrow border along both long sides, and some are left plain.

The four groups described above cover rather large pieces which were almost certainly part of the commercial tradition, but alongside this semi-industrial production there was a truly domestic group of embroidery for costume. Women's dresses were decorated at the neck bands, sleeves and skirt ends; men's costume would seem to be bought already embroidered using silver wire and commercially produced metallic braid. In this volume I have chosen not to include costume, so the only domestic pieces that fall within its scope are the embroidered

One leaf of an altar curtain, divided into fifteen rows of five squares, alternately containing a large or small pattern. The large ones are mainly animals or humans, the small ones set in a square are of birds, men, animals or flowers. The right-hand and bottom borders, of a meander with a carnation and a tulip, are original, the left-hand border was added later. The other leaf is in the Victoria & Albert Museum (T.24-1951). Epirus, about 1750.

sash ends, towels ends, small cushion covers and samplers. It is very difficult to distinguish the towel ends, the *peskiria*, from the much larger corpus of Ottoman work made throughout the empire, as in most cases they use the same patterns and techniques. There is, however, one particular pattern that can be described as Epirote, and that is the lady dressed in a wide renaissance skirt and small bodice, with a Venetian mob cap, set in a bower and flanked by two branches from which a rose and two leaves sprout. The woman always has her feet pointing outwards, as if the design was pounced from a folded-over drawing.

The sashes were made of one width of fine linen, about 40 cm wide and 120 cm long, worked in darning, split and satin stitch in bright dyed silks. Because the sashes would have been heavily used they tend to deteriorate, and when the fashion for such sashes ended, presumably with the universal acceptance of European costume from about 1870 onwards, the two decorated ends were cut off the sash and sewn together. When they are shown in museums in this state they are invariably described as cushion covers.

Left A composite panel made of the ends of three different scarfs. The end ones show a European lady in a hoop skirt wearing a tiara and cap. The other motifs are typically Turkish. Epirus, about 1800.

Right The two ends of a sash showing parrots. Epirus, about 1800.

11 Imagery and Pattern

The imagery of the island embroideries, as with all evolved folk art, is complicated; the processes by which it was developed have been forgotten and we are left with the objects themselves, and some knowledge of the history of the people and of the period in which they were made. A discussion of the visual aspects of the textiles is easy: one has merely to report what one sees; but to see the same textiles with the eyes of those who made them or for whom they were made, is not easy. Even the language in which we report what we see is different to that used by the makers and certainly the emotional significance of the names and terms has been lost. The textiles were a product of the culture around them, and it is therefore necessary to understand that culture, and how people lived within it, in order fully to see the embroideries and to read into them what the maker intended.

Before entering into the thorny ground of the derivation of patterns and designs, or into the even more contentious ground of their symbolism, it needs to be said that the largest part of all folk art is the copying and the occasional pragmatic adaptation of existing patterns. Not every craftsman was seized with an original inspiration that had to be translated into an object; in most instances new patterns were not desired, it was the known and familiar that was wanted and which had to be reproduced.

Having to embroider was a chore for most of the women and girls, but it was often the most pleasurable part of the long obligation of making clothes and domestic linen. In many cases it was enhanced by the thought that what they were labouring over was to be used in their marriage, or in one of the family or village ceremonies, which were great events within a regular, uneventful life. There are many songs that mention brides and grooms and the happy lives that will be 'lit up with gold and silver and flowers and sweet smelling herbs.' All of these ideas were worked into the embroideries that were to be used in the new married life.

In most cases folk embroideries are repetitive and predictable and

Two panels of a bed curtain. The centres and bottoms are worked with the spitha and the side borders with a compressed double leaf. Kos, about 1750.

147

eventually boring. It is the great virtue of Greek island work that in the surrounding sea of conventional embroidery - predictable Turkish work, rigid Mamluk work and formalised smart Italian work - Greek island embroiderers were able to produce a corpus of work that is rich and varied, drawing on all the surrounding traditions, and on some innate sense of pattern and order, so as finally to produce something new and different.

A central feature of much of the work is the use of two main patterns - the *platyfyllo*, the broad-leaf pattern of two large leaves set opposite each other, and the *spitha*, the spark or branch pattern, which is a linear design of a central spine with lateral radiating upward branches. Both patterns are worked in counted stitch and lend themselves to endless variations, which can be changes of the internal structure of the shapes, or of scale, or in the way they are used in combination and repetition. These two designs were named by Wace as the 'king' and 'queen' patterns, without any evidence that these were the local names. They do, however, reflect their prime importance, and because of the romance and nobility of the names themselves they helped considerably in promoting interest in Greek embroidery. The names were not initially used by any of his contemporaries, who called them the 'leaf' and the 'branch' patterns.

Both patterns were derived from imported textiles. The leaf is from woven textiles with a standard fold-over repeat, a feature common in Sassanian and Chinese weaving, later incorporated into Byzantine and Coptic fabrics. The branch pattern would be easier to embroider than weave, and first appears in Mamluk embroidery. It was extensively copied: in the west it appears in Maghrebi and Spanish work and in the east it is found in Turkish and central Asian work. The genius of the Aegean embroiderer was to see that variations of the two patterns could be used together, fitting into each other to create a new dense design. This idea breaks away from the Mamluk style of each distinct pattern always being used separately within rigid borders, introducing a sense of spontaneity and freedom into the work. Both designs are worked in counted stitches on a cloth held in the hand.

In Naxos a different type of counted work was developed, based on complicated, repeated geometric shapes covering the whole surface. The pattern was freely drawn onto the cloth, usually a series of circles and intersecting lines, which were then used to produce a bewildering variety of extravagant variations on a simple theme. The local embroiderer has skilfully changed a conventional Italian technique into something much more exciting. This over-all design technique is an amalgam of the Islamic formula of endlessly complicating a basic shape, and the Italian one of filling a surface with a pattern. The elaboration of a theme is carried further in Naxos than in any other European embroidery, and resembles Indonesian or African work. This artistic innovation is further enhanced by the technique of laying a monochrome floss silk in opposite directions in a conventional darning stitch, which gives an effect of two tones of the same colour, making

Above The top edge of a bed curtain, formed of two different panels each containing three columns of double-leaf patterns in three colours. The top edge has the basic pattern filled in with an angular pattern set above the double axe border. Amorgos, before 1750.

Right Part of a bed curtain panel, worked with a large octagon subdivided into a star and four diamonds, each shape filled with a developed Mamluk design. Naxos, about 1750.

p.48, 49

the use of other colours almost unnecessary. Not only were the over-all patterns developed and changed but even the retaining border patterns were seldom repeated, each embroiderer producing her own variation. There is, however, no particular imagery involved in this style of embroidery, the tradition was too strong to allow the imagination rather than the skill of the embroiderer to be developed.

p.86, 90

Once one enters the worlds of the other islands, imagination and invention becomes more evident. In the Cyclades a range of small human and animal forms were introduced into rather rigid over-all frameworks. The lines became very linear and stretched-out, being loosely worked over the surface in a range of pale colours, in complete contrast to the regular, compact Naxian style, which was aggressively monochrome and dark.

p.58

In Rhodes the impetus was to provide bed fittings for the patricians and the wealthy, and the decoration may initially have been based on the flattering conceit of using personal coats of arms as the main motif. As the tradition percolated down through society, as it always does, the coats of arms, which had very little relevance to the general population, slowly developed into forms with which they were more familiar, such as an urn. Perhaps the bed tents made for sale, with no particular family

p.165

purchaser in mind, merely required that the pattern look as if it were a coat of arms. This led to the final deterioration of the emblem into a clotted blob.

In the northern Dodecanese the basic pattern was a filled medallion, based on a motif seen in Turkish or European woven fabrics, akin to the guls in knotted rugs from the Caucasus and central Asia. In working these shapes, the general circular shape was preserved, but a variety of inner patterns were evolved and from their names we can see that the inspiration was from nature: almonds, pears and leaves, birds, and even common coins in circulation.

The Dodecanese tradition remained strict, and very few new forms were introduced into it, with the one great exception of the door of the Rhodian and Koan bed tent, where a separate panel was made which incorporated a door with single or multiple angular gables, based on an architectural model. The jambs are filled with the standard combined broad leaf and branch pattern, but the area within and without the gable bursts into a canvas of different motifs repeated exactly right and left. These come from many sources, mainly other textiles, tiles and carving, and are augmented and surrounded by many

p.6, 63, 67

Part of a Rhodian bed furnishing, showing the bottom of a tent panel and the edge of the valance with a large coat of arms. Rhodes, about 1720.

small motifs, introduced to fill in the background, sometimes clearly the result of an embroiderer being prompted by a vacant space to spontaneously fill it with a converted standard motif.

p.160

Some motifs are derived from patrician heraldry - the coats of arms, the lion looking over its shoulder, a small curvilinear lion, and other mythical beasts. The sparse double-headed eagle comes from Byzantine iconography, and the variety of fat birds from Islamic and Turkish decorative art, as do the formal medallions. The lady in the tower and the range of sailing ships come from renaissance Europe. The antlered

p.90, 93

deer comes from Ionian textiles, the little stocking-net-capped sailors from Skyros and the angular dog from the southern Cyclades. The professional atelier may not have had access to all these sources, but perhaps the lingua franca of embroidery was more universal than we imagine. If that is true, then the identification of textiles from their motifs will become even more contentious than it is now.

The final group is those small motifs used to fill out blank spaces: the single fleur-de-lys, the many versions of armorial crests and crosses, amongst which are an eight-pointed Hospitaller cross and a square-armed cross with a superimposed thin star, coming from a patrician

A man's sash showing a turbanned man holding a spray of flowers, with a block of seven flowers like a printed pattern. Samos, about 1850.

repertoire. The small irregular birds, the profusion of single stars and medallions, and the many forms of little humans would appear to come a from domestic tradition – humans in plebeian costume, armed men carrying bows, with and without arrows, sometimes carrying on their extended arm a shape that can be read as a hawk or falcon or even a cross, although this may just be an accident of the placing. Sometimes the men are shown mounted on horses or even, more surprisingly, on the heraldic leopards. The women are usually portrayed carrying flowers or domestic utensils.

The most interesting of these in-fill motifs are those developed patterns that almost become the signature of the atelier. The most distinctive of them is the cross made of five eight-pointed stars, where the bottom star has been omitted and a head, arms and legs have been added to make the cross into a skirted woman. Another unusal form is a bird shown facing the viewer, an unsuccessful attempt at realism which breaks away from the formal icon of the byzantine two-headed eagle. In this case the bird is shown in a very angular pose, with the tail feathers spread out as a skirt and the wings curling round the body on both sides.

Epirus was an unrivalled producer of embroidery. Apart from commercialism, this can be directly attributed to the mixture of populations and the independence of spirit that such a mix creates. Alongside the predictable Turkish repertoire we suddenly find in-trusions of human figures and touches of humour. The concentration of professional ateliers liberated the domestic embroiderer from having to copy a patrician tradition, and allowed a more vulgar style to be developed, primarily in the creation of small domestic pieces but also in local costume. The wedding bolster covers and bed sheets are the perfect examples of this tradition, being representations of the most important of all family ceremonies, the marriage.

p.158

p.43

Left Four borders from a cover sewn together to make a long strip. Three lengths have a pair of opposed partridges and the fourth pairs of a different bird worked in yellow. Siphnos, about 1750.

Above right A quarter of an Epirote wedding-bed cover showing the bride, groom and mounted best man in Venetian dress, she wearing a tiara and mobcap, the men with European tricornes, the Turkish attendant wearing a turban. The decoration is full of wedding symbols, the jug of pure water, peacocks, dogs and wild birds. Yanina, about 1720.

p.135

In a feudal society, particularly one under occupation, marriage emphasises the community and its persistence, and the creation of wider family links by which alliances are made and property is redistributed. All this is portrayed in the covers. The bride and groom are shown, sometimes a third significant personage is portrayed, either a father or a koumbaros, or less frequently a sister or servant of the bride. The class and wealth of the family are indicated either by the richness of the, sometimes the bride wears a crown with an aigrette trembler jewel and an inner velvet mob cap, the *skoufia*, or by the number of attendants and the fact that the figures are mounted on caparisoned horses. In one cushion the bride has three girl attendants and one male; in another the couple is flanked by a mounted grandee, each of whom is led by a walking groom. Because the Turkish costumes worn by both men and women can be confusing, one sees the same frock coat and inner tunic worn by both sexes, the only identification of sex is that all the women have a long black tress of hair, usually hanging to the left of the face.

The rest of the cushion and bolster covers are conventional, showing ewers with flowers, isolated sprays of flowers – carnations, hyacinths and tulips – pairs of birds and dogs, and even pairs of women-faced birds, harpies. The ewers and flowers are symbols of purity. I have never been able to discover the symbolism of the dogs; to say they represent fidelity is almost too trite to be right. The significance of the harpies has been lost. Elsewhere in Greece they are thought to be the Lion of St Mark, portraying the Serene Republic, but in this form they have deteriorated so much that it is almost an act of faith to see in them this Byzantine symbol of the second evangelist. I am sure that they are not the evil creature from classical literature and myth: they appear on too many domestic and ritual objects to be evil, and I do not think that they are naïve representations of cherubim. Angels are always portrayed quite differently in Epirote embroidery, so perhaps they are lions which have acquired human faces and have become representations of heavenly protection.

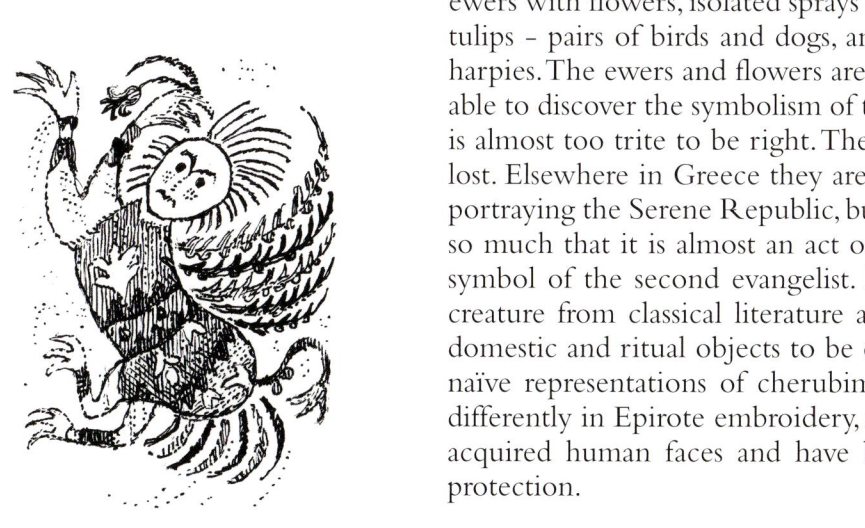

The last of the representational embroideries of Epirus are outside the Ottoman tradition, even though they still include the large tulip heads always considered as archetypal Turkish motifs. These are the long embroideries divided into five compartments, which have been earlier discussed and identified as altar frontals influenced by Venetian examples. The piece with five angels embroidered in the compartments and the other have a wonderful display - the first in the bottom border and the second in the five compartments - of the whole repertoire of mythical and conventional motifs, worked in a very immediate way which is not at all hackneyed, giving a feeling of these particular designs being worked for the first time.

Another piece of church embroidery, a domestic piece made to be presented to the church, is the small fragment of Cycladic work which is sadly incomplete. It is worked in darning and satin stitch and alongside the representations of birds and three winged snakes there is p.54 a blazon from an unidentified coat of arms, and also a small picture rather like an icon. It shows Christ floating above Peter in his boat, telling him to cast his net into the sea to gather the miraculous draught of fishes.

Skyran embroidery is very direct. The images deal with daily life: working with the sea accounts for the many vessels riding the sea full p.97 of fish; the social order is shown in the many representations of officials and their entourages, and family life is shown in the celebratory textiles of marriages and betrothals. Religion is occasionally referred to with a cross on a child's headband, but it is much commoner to find images drawn from superstition - the witches and harpies, the fantastic beasts and the half-humans. Spectacularly, it is the cockerel that represents the p.96 spirit of the people, the image of bold independence.

The seventeenth and eighteenth century embroideries of Crete are well known mainly because they belong to a more familiar idiom, being copies of an established Italian tradition. They are skirt borders p.106,108,110 and this has somehow diminished their importance. If the same work had been done on more prestigious articles, such as altar frontals or marriage cloths, they would be far more appreciated. It is interesting to note that a number of them were eventually converted into copes and church cloths.

With an established repertoire the Cretan embroiderer was still able to introduce into the work two separate local images. The first is a formal one of converting certain shapes into more appropriate images: the gorgon with two tails is given a full crown, the tails are changed into the edge of a cloak and the figure becomes the Panagia, the Virgin Mary, or at least the Queen of Heaven. Crete is full of Venetian buildings encrusted with commemorative tablets and coats of arms, and families with claims to these devices would incorporate them into their domestic embroideries, changing the gorgon's breast into a shield with a chequered pattern, or a shield with three coins, and the breast of the eagle changes to a blazon with a bar.

The second version fills the established pattern with local motifs: a

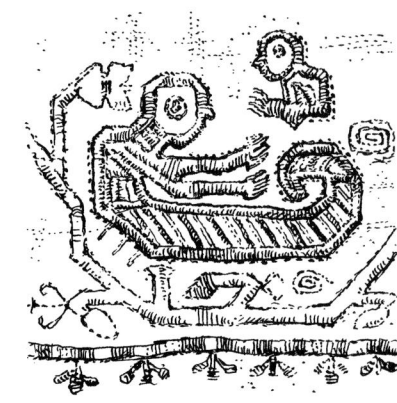

154

p.106

wedding couple, a dance with a man playing the violin and a host of mythical beasts, dragons, snakes, the woman-faced bird, dogs, birds, the *aspis*, and a variety of little homunculi who hang on the tendrils of plants and around the bases of the vases. The shapes change, the two-headed eagle loses its imperial splendour and deteriorates into a domestic fowl or a meaningless shape, the formal vase becomes a baseless collection of flowers and branches.

p.116

When the revival of Cretan embroidery starts at the end of the nineteenth century, a new repertoire of images is introduced that had not existed before – St George on horseback, spiders, simplified versions of lions reduced to little kittens, and even caterpillars that were once dragons.

The whole corpus of Greek island embroideries shows how a native tradition can be developed which is primarily based on a broad variety of introduced elements from three or four differing cultures. These elements are fused one with the other over time, and changed to incorporate native images and themes. They are adapted not only to the everyday usage of decorated objects but also to the local culture and mythology.

Detail from a cover showing three men in a sailing boat with birds in the rigging. This piece shows the remnants of captions in Ottoman script. Sporades, about 1750.

156

12 The Etymology of Greek Embroidery

Once upon a time there was an embroideress who had pupils, and she taught them to embroider designs on all sorts of cloth. The embroideress was good and very capable, and embroidered shirts, towels, napkins, table cloths, kerchiefs, bed tents with their doors, sheets, cushion covers and all sorts of clothing.

The Tale of Yavrouda, Zarraftis MS.

Very little embroidery has survived from classical Greece and Rome, although the craft certainly existed, even if it was neither as universal nor as valued as weaving. From the surviving examples of much later textiles, the Hellenistic and Roman textiles of Egypt, we must assume that the main method of applying pattern to a textile was weaving at the loom. This was done either by changing the weft colour or by introducing extra coloured wefts, as had been done in China, Sassanian Persia, Egypt and eventually Byzantium.

There are innumerable references to weaving in the classics, from Homer's Penelope to the aristocratic ladies of Euripides who were responsible for weaving the decorative and ornamental borders onto plain stuff that had been woven by slaves and servants. The whole concept of weaving and preparing materials for weaving was extensively drawn upon for describing the world and the forces that controlled it – the Fates spun and wove and then cut the finished cloth of life. The references to embroidery are few and, I believe, have been misunderstood.

The word used in classical Greek that is usually translated as embroidery is *poikillein*, which on examination would appear more exactly to mean 'to make multi-coloured'. Professor Wace, in discussing this point, reinforces this belief, suggesting that it is not until Byzantine times that embroidery was introduced into the Eastern Empire. The Roman world had a longer history of embroidery, and there are two phrases that refer to and classify embroidery. The first is *plumarium opus*, that work with a pattern like, or in the manner of, feathers; derived from *pluma* – a feather. The second is *phrygium opus*, work in the Phrygian style, most probably meant to be exclusively that of decorating with silver and gold. Marica Monte Santo, in *L'Isola dei*

Gigli, further defines plumarium opus as embroidery using any flat stitch, and phrygium opus as that using a cross stitch, indicating that the metallic thread or decoration was applied and held to the cloth by an overlaid cross stitch, as is still done today in Turkey, Iran and India.

It is interesting to note that in Mamluk Egypt there are references, particularly in the Geniza documents, to textiles with feathering on their borders. The word used is *murayyash*, derived from *risha*, a feather. In the absence of Pharaonic embroidery it could be assumed that embroidery in Egypt starts in the Graeco-Roman period, and that the word used was a literal translation of the Latin *plumarium*, the Mamluks and Arabs using the same basic root word of a feather.

I am a believer in the persistence of custom and culture in language, and always investigate words as indicators of social change. The only survivals of the classic *poikillein* in modern Greek is *poikillo*, to adorn, and *poikilia*, a variety or an assortment, which reinforces Wace's proposition that the classical word refers to decoration and not exclusively to embroidery. The word that is used in later Greek for embroidery is *kentima*, derived from the verb *kento*, which originally meant 'to prick or sting like a bee', and was first used in the sense of pouncing. The word eventually came to mean, as it does in demotic Greek today, to embroider. It is the word used in Hellenistic Egypt and later in Byzantium for embroidery.

The word used in the islands is *ploumizo*, and the word for a pattern is *ploumi*, with a diminutive *plomaki*, as used in the fourth line of the poem of 1485 by Emmanuel Georgillas, quoted at the front of this book. It is also used in the first lines of *Yavrouda*, one of the Dodecanese fairy tales collected in Asphendiou in Kos and edited by Professor R.M.Dawkins, quoted at the head of this chapter. The list of articles to be embroidered in both quotations is virtually those of the items that were still being embroidered up to 1850, when the habit of domestic embroidery started to die out in the islands.

Ploumizo is obviously derived from the Latin *pluma*. It was first used in Greek in the sixth century AD, and was later widely diffused into Greek spoken in the Aegean after 1204. The new Latin aristocracy brought with them new styles, techniques and products, incidentally introducing into the language new words for crafts, processes and objects. This new vocabulary covered all phases of life, the sea, religion, law and textiles; this last, which is pertinent to this study, produces *sperveri* and *xombli*, which are not obvious, and others which are, such as *kortina*, and *porta*.

Sperveri describes an article that had not existed in the Greek world but which had been introduced from medieval Europe. It is the hanging that was used in patrician families to isolate the bed from the rest of the room, to permit some privacy but also to insulate it from the cold of unheated rooms. The word is derived from the word for a fishing net and for a sparrow-hawk, *espervier* in French and *sparviere* in Italian: the drape around the bed must have been thought to look like a sparrow-hawk with its wings outstretched. The name was also used

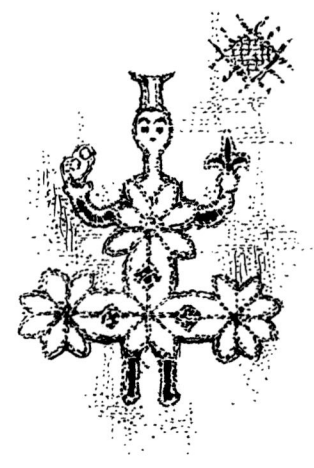

Page 156: A wall hanging for a bed. Originally the lower quarter would have been undecorated, hanging behind the bed. When the usage changed, the bottom quarter was embroidered by a much less skilled hand in a perfunctory version of the original. Siphnos, about 1750.

for a fishing net of the same shape. In Godefroy in 1380 it is the word that is used to describe the ensemble of pieces of cloth that form the bed, by 1480 the word had become sparver in English and *spawari* in High German. When it was introduced into the Aegean, and that must have been well before 1485, the word had become *sperveri* or even *perveri*.

The bed tent has already been described at length, and not only did the word for the tent itself come into the language but also the words for the tent door, the *porta*, the word for the ensemble of the door, the *mostra* and the word for the design above the gable, the *koumpaso*. It had been used by Boccaccio in one of his *Novellas* in 1400, where he refers to a cover, a *coltre*, worked with a pattern of compartments filled with large pearls, *lavorato a certi compassi di perle grossissime*.

Xombli is used now in Astypalaia for both a sampler, a direct derivation from the Latin *exemplum*, and for that range of stitches or patterns taken from a sampler. Embroidery patterns in Greece today are divided into two types, *grafta*, which are those drawn on the cloth before starting to embroider, and those called *metrita* or *xombliasta*, which are those based on counted stitches or copied from a sampler.

The words derived from Arabic, particularly in Mamluk usage, are more difficult to be sure about. They may either have entered the language directly or later through the Ottomans, who acquired it first. Among these are *makrama*, *mandil* and *peshkir*, The introductions also include words for dyes such as *baqqam* and *boya*, and the words for furniture and house fittings that have been mentioned earlier.

Words from Ottoman Turkish abound and are best observed in the Sporades, which were very influenced by the Ottomans. The most interesting words that do survive are those concerned with building, such as *bolmes* and *mussandira*, both explained earlier.

Research into language can be used as a dating method to show how fashion and usage change are reflected in words. They also reflect the social and political changes in a culture. Demotic Greek allows one to observe these changes more than any other language in Europe.

An embroidered strip for a table, adapting an Ottoman velvet pattern, using metal thread and silk, in overlapping stem stitch. Cycladic, about 1750.

159

13   Materials

Embroidery was virtually the only means of artistic expression and domestic decoration available to the islanders to enrich their daily lives. It had the advantage that it was relatively cheap to do. Painting was reserved for the Church and for the holy icons executed by priests or acolytes, carving was a trade occupation and pottery involved considerable capital expenditure.

Houses were white both inside and out - the fashion for painting houses blue in the Dodecanese, which slowly spread to the other islands, was very late, a gesture against being occupied. Wood, used inside the house for the partition and balcony, for cupboards and for the range of chests and boxes, was left plain, with only a little carving in the Skyros houses. The decoration in the house, therefore, apart from the holy pictures and the coloured plates on shelves, came from the textiles and clothing hung on wall-hooks when not being worn, so colour in the room came from the embroidered bed curtains, cushions, bed spreads and valances.

Domestic embroidery was made only by the women of the family, from the oldest grandmother to girls aged seven onwards. In the richer families the women spent a great deal of their leisure time with needles in hand. A Jesuit visitor to Naxos in 1643 reports in his journal: *'Les dames de la ville...sortent rarement de la maison. Elles ne savent lire ni écrire, se contenant d'apprendre bien à coudre et faire toute sorte d'ouvrage sur la toile.'* Presumably these were patrician Latin ladies: a Jesuit priest would be unlikely to be visiting the Greeks. It is interesting to note that even these leisured ladies sewed, presumably making most of their own clothes. The women of the poorer families would embroider, although it is likely that most of their time was spent at the loom or making the fabric up into clothes, rather than decorating them.

Even the island professionals who embroidered to order were women, whereas in larger centres such as Yanina or Istanbul they would have been men. Women were responsible for instructing the girls in dress-making and embroidery, teaching both stitching techniques and patterns. The industrial production of embroideries in large centres

Six panels from a most impressive bed tent which would not have had a separate door, indicating that it was a special order for a specific family. The panels show coats of arms of different sizes, but clearly all worked in the same atelier in a rather open manner. Rhodes, about 1700.

161

such as Kos and Rhodes was carried out in small ateliers staffed by men, who could have been Greeks, Turks, Armenians and Jews. The professional would have concentrated on men's clothing and trade textiles, particularly any using braid and gold.

Traditionally embroidery is associated with the preparation of the dowry, and any grand article of embroidery is invariably called a wedding piece. This may be so, but much embroidery was made for other festive occasions and celebrations as well. Dowry contracts show that very few new pieces were handed on, it was mostly used pieces from the family store of bedding, household linen and clothing. One particular dowry list includes a 'peacock blue shift' and the donor adds a comment: 'whenever I ask for the peacock blue one she must lend it to me for as long as I live.' It is reckoned that more than half the value of all the items inherited or donated by dowry contracts or wills are clothing or textiles; clothing and bed linen could be passed on and used again and again.

The materials used were linen and cotton for the ground fabric, and all embroidery was in silk. Later the use of metal-covered silk or cotton, filé, or occasionally thin strips of metal was introduced, and later still one finds wool being used. These new materials were being produced in the Ottoman empire and were first used in the grand ateliers of Tepebashi in Istanbul, where very high quality dival work was produced in industrial quantities. The fashion gradually spread throughout from Bosnia to central Asia.

At the time of the embroideries discussed in this book, all the materials were produced locally. Linen was grown all over the eastern Mediterranean from ancient times; the main centre must have been Pharaonic Egypt, which had an enormous consumption, but there are references to flax being grown all along the coast from Greece to the mouth of the Nile. It must have been both *Linum humile* and *Linum usitatissimum*; both produced a strong, long fibre that allowed either fine or coarse cloth to be woven. Cotton was a later introduction, most probably after the conquests of Alexander the Great into India. It was *Gossypium herbaceum* and was seen as a wonder by both the Greeks and the Romans; Herodotus describes it as a tree which grew wild, bearing a wool rather than a fruit. The plant described by Pliny is almost certainly *Gossypium arboreum*, which was never grown in the islands. Cotton gradually replaced the production of linen, mainly because its production avoided retting, a process very dependent on abundant water. It also produced a fabric as strong as linen but also a finer, gossamer-like textile.

The most perfect of all fibres, silk, was the last introduced into the area. It came from India and China and was known long before any was imported. Silk is the fine covering of the larva of the mulberry leaf moth, *Bombyx mori*, which can be drawn out and made into a thread of as many single strands as necessary. Although silk was used in the West from the first century BC, it was initially obtained, according to Lucan, from woven fabric imported from China: the word for silk, *seres* was the name for China. The woven silk was unpicked by the Egyptians into single threads which were then used used for reweaving into a decorative coloured border on a plain fabric or, sometimes, even completely rewoven into a looser silk fabric. The valuable silk was either mixed with linen or cotton to produce the union fabrics known as *semisirika*, half silk, as opposed to the all silk fabric, *olosirika*. Lucan even suggests that in Egypt single threads were pulled from woven Chinese silk imported via the Lebanon, both to lighten the texture of that material and also to provide a supply of spun silk. In *Pharsalia*, X, 141, he says: 'The fabric of Sidon, tightly woven by the Chinese, has been separated by the craftsman of the Nile with his needle, loosening the web.'

The earliest references supposed to refer to silk are Aristotle's mentions of the diaphanous garments worn by the women of Kos, and the transparency of Amorgine garments. If it is silk that he refers to then it is to the 'unloosening, reeling off and weaving' of imported fabric, and should not be taken to mean that silk was produced in Kos at that time; not even as has been suggested, from the wild silk-moth, like Indian tussore. If diaphanous garments were produced in Kos, then they were of fine cotton. The Assyrian bombyx that Pliny mentions is more likely to be the Greek *mpampak* or Turkish *pamuk*, both of which mean cotton and not silk. A similar word means cotton in many near eastern languages and is not like the word for silk in any of them, which is always a variant of an introduced word.

It was only in the second century BC, under the Emperor Wu Ti, that the Silk Route from China to the eastern edge of Persia was opened. There are no references to silk in the classical world before the third century AD. Because it was a costly imported article Heliogabalus in 215 AD decreed that it was only to be worn by the Imperial family, and later in 404 AD Justinian forbade its use altogether. The pressure to wear silk was so great in the Eastern Empire that Constantine set up weaving sheds in the *gynacea* of the imperial palace in the fourth century for all fabrics, including silk, and Constantinople became the centre of the new industry of silk weaving.

This new industry spread very quickly to Alexandria, Tyre, Antinoe and Damascus. All produced great textiles, only fragments of which have survived. This demand for silk and the new knowledge of how to cultivate silk worms meant that its production became a new industry, and mulberries were planted wherever they could be grown – in the islands, in Attica, Boetia and the Peloponese, which subsequently became known as the Morea from the quantity of mulberry trees grown there, taking its name from the Frankish word for mulberry, *morus*.

In 1071 Georgios Antiochenos, the Admiral of Roger II, is chronicled as having captured workers who could both rear silk worms and produce cloth, and transported them from Thebes, the area that was known as *morokampos*, the mulberry field', to the court in Sicily. Roger founded the Hotel de Tiraz in Palermo to produce woven fabrics

similar to those at the Fatimid Dar AtTiraz in Alexandria. However, there is strong evidence that the silk industry was flourishing in Sicily at least two centuries before that date; Sicily was already exporting both raw silk and finished cloth, *siqlatun*, throughout the Mediterranean. Silk remained important in the islands and in mainland Greece; Saewulf in his travels of 1102 mentions visiting Andros, where 'Sindals and samits and other stuffs of silk' were made, and in 1160 Benjamin of Tuleda tells of the large Jewish community in Thebes who were the most eminent manufacturers of silk and purple cloth in Greece. In 1198 there is a reference to the Emperor Alexius III sending forty pieces of silk to the Sultan of Angora as a gift, all of which had been made in Thebes.

This movement into Sicily, whenever it happened, can be seen as the first step in the creation of the great silk industry that was to spread from Sicily to Lucca, after Angevin rule was installed in 1266, and after that to Genoa and Venice and then throughout Europe.

Although silk continued to be produced and woven in Greece, the industry was no longer as exclusive as it had been. The Popes who had sent orders for silk vestments to their Orthodox colleagues in the East, of which there is a very long list, now obtained them from the new manufacturers in Italy.

The demand for silk was so high from the thirteenth century onwards that no single producing area was able to satisfy the new demand. There are records of Luccan and Genoese merchants travelling to the Caspian for raw silk, to Ghilan, Georgia and Gandja, and taking the silk overland to Batoum and shipping it from there back to Genoa. Even when silk was being produced all over the Middle East the Greek archipelago remained a primary producer. Tinos and Andros were the main centres in the Aegean: in 1563 Tinos was one of the most populated islands, with 9000 inhabitants, and silk was its staple product and wealth, so much so that all the taxes to the Ottoman Empire from that island were paid in silk.

The mechanised production of silk woven products in the Aegean can be dated to about 1480, when refugees from the silk mercers' guild in Genoa fled to Chios and manufactured woven silk on an industrial scale. The government of Genoa was so concerned at this move from Genoa to the area where the raw silk was produced that they forced the Mahona in Chios to return the silk masters to Genoa. However, the manufacture of silk cloth had been established and by 1550 Chios was importing raw silk to satisfy their industrial capacity, as local production was no longer large enough. Chios became the main exporter of a range of silk weaves, including satins, velvets and damasks with silver and gold, throughout the Ottoman Empire.

Even into the beginning of the eighteenth century the islands, or the Archipelago, as it was then called, produced large quantities of linen, cotton and silk.

The trade in these products and in some other finished goods, woven linen and cotton stockings, continued from the middle of the fifteenth century until the beginning of the nineteenth. The Napoleonic Wars

and the steady progress of industrialization in the west made the commerce no longer profitable; the production of silk ceased, the mulberries were uprooted and more profitable crops such as almonds and hazel nuts were planted. The trade with the east, particularly to the Ottoman empire, continued, although the volumes gradually decreased as imported cheaper cloths became available from Europe. Céleste David, writing in 1824, says that the Chians relied too much on their past reputation, and by reducing the quality of their products had lost their market share. So they gradually turned from being producers to being traders, selling into their export markets products they bought elsewhere.

The end of the embroidery tradition can be traced almost to that time, when there was no locally produced silk and imported silk was too expensive to be used. This, combined with the change in fashions dictating that women should now wear the new garments, meant that old style clothes, although possibly still being worn, were no longer being made. The great period in which these embroideries were made must then be between 1650 and 1800, with the tradition dying first in those islands nearest the mainland, such as the Cyclades, or in those where industrialization came early, such as Chios, but lingering on in the furthest islands such as Amorgos, Karpathos and Astypalaia.

After the creation of the New Greece and the introduction of a universal schooling system, when both boys and girls were sent to the public schools, embroidery was taught to the girls as a craft subject. The Royal Hellenic School of Needlework was founded in Athens in 1896 and distributed to schools pattern books with classical patterns and adaptations of folk patterns. There was a strong revival of Cretan patterns in Crete about 1900; the old feather stitch was used extensively on new embroideries, and even old pieces of Turkish, Bulgarian and other Greek embroideries were further embellished with the new embroidery. Wace has a reference to a lady in Algiers who had set up an atelier to produce embroideries in the style of Crete, which were collected by tourists as original pieces.

p.116
p.166

Linen was woven in the home or bought from a local weaver. It came in standard widths of 40–50 cm in pieces of 15 'piches' (about 30 feet/10 metres). Cotton was produced in a greater range of weights, right down to a gossamer-like material which was used for scarfs, particularly the machramades of Astypalaia, and for the very light curtains of Siphnos.

p.79
p.156

Both linen and cotton were imported from other islands and from the Turkish mainland, particularly the fine linen and cotton which had bands of silk warp on both sides. This fabric was in demand for the poukamiso of Skyros and Kalymnos and for the lighter working shirts of the islands, as was the Turkish crepe, *gömlek*. Silk yardage was imported from Constantinople and Chios, although this was not commonly used other than for the women's short waistcoat. Some silk thread had always been imported, usually those colours that were not dyed locally, even when the islands were centres of silk production.

p.73

166

14 Techniques

The island woman in the Aegean was responsible for every aspect of the life in the house, while the man's responsibility was external. He had a trade or a skill which he pursued; he kept up the fabric of the house, and if there were any animals, as was most common, he looked after them. The woman looked after the children and very often her husband's parents as well, cooked and made the clothes and the materials from which the clothes were made. Cloth was made on a flat loom, called a *krevata* or *krevataria*, and it was usual for each house to have a loom. These were considered as part of the family property and are frequently mentioned in wills, where the loom, all its equipment and various implements are detailed as part of the inheritance, even to the length of fabric still on the loom.

The stitches

The technique of embroidery in the islands was that universal one diffused throughout Europe and the Near East, although the islands did invent a number of stitches – the Rhodian and Astypalaian cross stitches and the elaborate Cretan feather stitch are the most spectacular of these.

The repertoire of stitches used in the islands is divided into two groups, *metrites* or counted, and *graftes*, or designed stitches. Counted stitches are worked by counting threads horizontally and vertically on the ground fabric; they can as easily be worked on fabric held either in the hand or set on a frame or tambour. In working cross stitch the fabric would be filled with the first arm of the cross stitch, with the second added later.

The names given to the different stitches vary not only from one group of islands to another but even within one island, where neighbouring villages call the same stitch by quite different names. Argenti, in his book *Costumes of Chios*, gives eight different names for cross stitch in that island and that one of them, *gazi*, can mean cross stitch, running or even double running in different parts of Chios – all

This cloth is Bulgarian and originally had a plain ground with twelve shield patterns set around the sides. When embroidery was reintroduced into Crete such pieces were filled in with traditional Cretan patterns, but in a way that was unknown in old pieces. The central medallion of a man on a donkey with a new moon is a favourite new motif. Reworked about 1900.

this confusion in an island that is not particularly noted for its embroidery. This means that although the lists given below identify the generally accepted names for the various stitches, there are likely to be very dramatic differences in some regions, proving that it is not possible to be dogmatic about the names, as it is about most of the techniques of embroidery.

The main counted stitches, *metrites,* are: *perasti* – darning, *gazoti* – double running, *stavro velonia* – cross stitch, *kamvas* – canvas or cross stitch, *isi* – surface filling, *garti* – long-armed cross, *playasti* – half cross, *fteroti* – feather, *dipli kentia* – double stitch or brick, and *loksia* – couched.

Designed or sketched stitches, *graftes,* follow a pattern drawn on the fabric, usually freehand, and not necessarily followed exactly. They are usually worked on a frame, which may be held in the hand or a larger table-frame at which the embroiderer would sit to work. Large pieces of more than one width of material would be tacked together initially and the pattern drawn overall, then unpicked and worked separately. When the finished strips are completed and re-sewn together it is not unusual and hardly surprising that they do not always match exactly.

The main sketched stitches, *graftes,* are: *anachyti* – satin, *fouskoti* – satin, *stromatsenia* – satin, *astachoti* – stem stitch, *seiritsa* – chain stitch, *alysidoti* – chain, *kasinaki* – chain, only Epirus, *psarokokkalo* – herring-bone, *dichaloti* – split, *natouralisia* – running stitch, *agagiotainas* – running stitch, *psiphiti* – brick, single or double, and *pisovelonia* – back stitch.

Pouncing is seldom used. I have only seen evidence of it in pieces that are copies of Italian work. This raises the possibility that island Italianate work was worked on imported cloth drawn and prepared in Italy. This would certainly explain the difference in the quality of the base linen found in this group of work. Some Italianate work is made on scraps sewn together which would not have been likely with an imported article but would be acceptable as local work copying it. Both methods may easily have been used at the same time at different levels of society.

An unfinished sleeve showing how the pattern is laid. The first arm of every cross stitch is placed, to be followed with the second arm. This is the way that samplers are worked to show patterns rather than stitches. Nisyros, about 1800.

Three other categories of stitches are used: *chyta*, with drawn thread work; those used to join edges or to make gussets; and the last is the couched stitch used in Karpathos and Kasos.

The drawn thread work stitches, *chytes* are: *trypito* – button hole, *ploumia* – needle weaving, *tylichtiko* – cross retaining, and *kangelloti* – cross. Drawn thread work is used for the broad bands at the ends of hand towels, or for small areas on larger pieces. It is usually white, except in Astypalaia and the Ionian Islands where it is also worked in blue and red.

The joining stitch is either the *psarangathi*, a feather stitch spread over the edge of two pieces of material laid side by side or the *kangelaki*, little grill, an insertion stitch like a lace bride, sometimes thickened with a buttonhole stitch.

The third stitch – the couched stitch – is only found in pieces attributed to Karpathos and Kasos, although it may exist elsewhere. It is used particularly on the short broad sleeve of the poukamiso. The stitch is a laid couched stitch made by holding the soft floss silk or a light silk cord in one hand above the fabric and twisting it firmly, causing it to twist on itself; the twisted strand is then placed in the required pattern and is fixed onto the fabric. The couching thread is on a needle held in the other hand below the fabric and the stitch is worked from below. This is worked with either a single or double strand of silk, usually in a different colour, but the over stitch is pulled so hard that the second colour cannot be seen. The final appearance is of an applied braid with none of the couching showing. The back of the embroidery shows a very regular ladder pattern of the couching silk, with the occasional short end or knot of the surface-laid silk being passed to the back of the ground material.

This technique is usually called *stromeni* or *strosti* and is not recognised elsewhere. The effect of the laid couched stitch is wonderfully opulent and extremely economical of silk. It is, however, extremely difficult to do in a disciplined way.

Needle weaving has a vocabulary of its own, with each pattern having its own name. Again Argenti identifies nearly two hundred different names used in Chiote villages alone. Bebilla stitch is used extensively to make a trimming for garments. It is most evident in the Sporades as a substitute lace trim for the elaborate poukamiso sleeve ends and neck openings. Bebilla was worked with a needle; in Skyros it is *kompos tis velonias* – a needle knot, or *kompos psariotikos* – fisherman's knot, now sometimes worked with a crochet hook.

Bebilla is described as being the same as the Turkish *oya*. The word means 'a distraction' and is a splendid description of the work. Oya is made with a tatting shuttle, with a crochet needle or even as a hand-knotted macrame. Greek bebilla is a needle lace and oya is not necessarily so. Both traditions have now become so mixed that the many patterns of the Turkish Aegean coast, and the equally large range of fancy names and silly attributions, are accepted in both traditions. The Greek tradition, with a limited range of patterns, more closely

resembles the European tradition of needle lace used for trimming.

The unique Rhodian and Astypalaian cross stitches are both fat raised stitches standing proud of the ground cloth. When they are worked with thick floss silk an effect of a voided velvet is acheived, which must have been the intention. Rhodian stitch is formed by the first arm of the cross laid in toto for the whole motif in the different directions that the pattern requires. This first arm is laid close to the ground fabric and pulled tightly onto it. The second arm is then worked loosely in the conventional manner, with the needle being given a slight final twist to make the untwisted floss bunch up. It has been suggested that the second arm might have been laid over a straw or thin strip of wood in a simple velvet technique, but there is no evidence of this. The labour required to work this way would have been abandoned quite quickly, particularly as twisting gives the same effect. Astypalaian cross differs in that the second arm is not worked into the basic fabric but is anchored onto the tightly laid first arm, giving an even richer velvet effect.

The samplers of Astypalaia show exactly how this stitch is worked. The pattern is shown giving only the first arm, indicating clearly the direction of the stitch. The second arm, in either technique, would then be placed in the opposite direction. This is critical because the pattern is worked so tightly that the only sense of internal pattern is derived from the way in which the untwisted floss silk catches the light. As Rhodian patterns developed and became denser, the detail of the design becomes less clear, making the directional laying of both arms more critical.

Samplers are more common in the islands than on the mainland. The Astypalaian name *xombli*, derived from the Latin 'exemplum', has spread all over Greece. The range of counted stitches, *xombliasta*, implies that they are copied from a sampler. The first sampler gives a range of fourteen main dixos designs and fourteen smaller subsidiary motifs, one row of the 'little fish' sleeve pattern and three frieze sleeve patterns. The second sampler only gives sleeve patterns: six friezes of different widths, each with the outer borders, six sleeve band patterns, one of which is

p.150, 165

Above A skirt border worked in an adaptation of an Italian design. The vase with plants has had human faces added to every circular shape, and this alternates with a gorgon and tail. The reverse shows how Cretan feather stitch looks on the back. Crete, about 1720.

Right The end of a hand towel, vagioli, from Astypalaia. It is worked in cross and button-hole stitch on a drawn thread ground, with the reverse showing how the stitches are laid. It imitates the woven towels of central Italy, and the patterns are Byzantine, Venetian and include family heraldic motifs. Compare with the illustration at the top of page 55. Astypalaia, about 1800.

the 'little fish' and another the full-tailed bird. On both samplers the patterns are unfilled; they are carried out in running stitch, one giving the first arm of the cross stitch only and the second one the outline of the frieze designs.

The sampler from the V&A Museum shows a range of dixos patterns in running stitch, but more economically shows only half of each dixos. The rest of the sampler is filled with versions of the main Astypalaian designs: ships, mounted animals and opposed birds.

Narrow lengths of material were joined either being sewn selvedge to selvedge or with an inserted narrow woven ribbon, usually a weave of alternate red and yellow stripes. The most common inserts were crocheted but fabric strips, industrial ribbon and even Milanese lace were also used. These lengths were commonly used with white work, for large counterpanes and bench covers. In Crete they were used with the *colletti* as inserts for the strips of recycled woven materials. The crocheted strips, *aratzidelles*, from the Italian *reticella*, copied milanese or bobbin lace.

The production of lace was limited; it was mainly *kopanelli* – bobbin lace – and a little lacis work. The few examples of lace that are called Greek are said to have been made in Melos; one piece in the Benaki so attributed is cushion lace which must be from an ecclesiastical garment, such as the flounce of an alb. It is composed of eight scenes set out in a frieze; the two central squares are: an Annunciation with the Virgin in a curtained bed with a winged Archangel on her left, and two angels hovering over a church. The other designs in the frieze are standard Aegean motifs, the double-headed eagle, sailors in a boat, and a mermaid holding up her double tail. A very pleasant combination of ecclesiastical and secular, a very common trait in the islands.

Dyeing

Most island embroidery is on bleached white or natural linen or cotton, while the embroidery is in polychrome silk, although a lot of white on white is found. Silk produced locally would have been dyed domestically. However, by as early as 1800 much of the silk thread would have been commercially spun and dyed and imported from the Ottoman world, or even from France and Italy.

In the catalogue for the Fitzwilliam Exhibition in 1906 Wace gives a list of the vegetable sources for dyeing silk. It is a short list and he developed the subject considerably in his introduction to the Burlington Fine Arts Exhibition in 1914, drawing on the information that Sibthorp had collected, which Walpole quotes in his *Memoirs relating to European and Asiatic Turkey*. I take the liberty of drawing from that section, with acknowledgments to Sibthorp, Walpole and Wace.

> **red**: *krimizi*. Kermes, the gall formed on the oak by the small insect (*Coccus ilicis*) that grows on the holm oak (*Quercus coccifera*).

rizari. The root of the madder plant (*Rub peregrina*). This dye was known to the ancient Greeks (Herodotus, Hippocrates, Dioscorides and Pliny).

komaria. A red dye is obtained from the root of the arbutus shrub (*Arbutus unedo).*

platanos. The roots of the plane tree (*Platanus orientalis*) yield red.

blue: *loulaki.* Indigo. This is not produced locally but is imported from the east as an article of commerce.

yellow: *ligaria.* The leaves of the ligaria (*Agnus castus*) give yellow.

chrysoxulon. Fustic, Xante fustic or Venetian sumach (*Rhus cotinus*). The wood of this tree yields a fine orange yellow.

chamelaiai or *himero herokalo.* (*Daphne oleoides* and *Daphne dioica*).

omioplevron. Mullein or Shepherd's Staff (*Thapsia villosa*).

ladzicheri, or *apeilirias.* Buckthorn. The unripe berries of this tree (*Rhamnus catharticus minor*) yield a yellow dye.

foudara or *gouthoura.* A yellow is obtained from the leaves of St. John's Wort (*Hypericum coris*).

trountzi. The flowers of Oxalis (*Oxalis comiculata*) give a yellow. *galatsida.* A kind of spurge, species uncertain.

green: *onitza* or *psillistra.* Fleabane (*Inula-Erigeron graveolens*). This is the only plant yielding green, which is usually obtained by mixing indigo with Daphne.

purple: *myrtia.* The berries of Myrtle (*Myrtus communis*) give the colour.

vatos. The colour is from blackberry (*Rubus fruticosus*) fruit.

brown: *valanidi.* This is the acorn cup of the Valonia oak (*Quercus aegilops*). Shades vary according to the strength of the bath.

black: This colour is obtained by dyeing silk already dyed with valonia, then with vitriol or sulphate of copper.

This is not in any way an exclusive list, as dyes can be obtained from a range of natural materials; most dyers devised their own method to get the colours they required. The international trade in dyes is ancient, coming since antiquity from India and the east beyond. They were in use in Egypt from the fifth century AD and might have been in the Aegean soon after.

Hatzimichaili, in her book on Skyros, mentions that some dyeing from local materials is still done and states that on Amorgos the red is derived from a red lichen, *Rocella tinctoria*, and on Karpathos the green is made from another lichen, *R. viridis.* The yarn is first soaked in alum, or in a solution of pomegranate skin or walnut husk, then dyed to the colour required. The red is *rizari*, which was grown extensively in Skyros, but later came from Kymi.

Blue is obtained by dissolving indigo or washing blue, *loulaki*, in the water in which wool has been washed, and then by steeping the yarn for eight days in the water in the sun; and dark brown by steeping the yarn in water in which walnut husks have been boiled. In this case there is no need to use alum, as the walnut husk has the same effect as alum. This method should only take a couple of hours to dye the yarn.

Black is obtained by steeping yarn that has already been dyed dark brown in a solution made by boiling sappan or logwood (*Caesalpinia sappan*). The Arabic and later Turkish word is *baqqam*. This wood was imported as small logs from India, and it produces a fugitive range of reds and dark browns. The instructions continue that if this does not produce a black strong enough then you boil the yarn with 'black dye', which I think is iron sulphate. Finally she explains that a pretty black is obtained by first dying the yarn yellow.

It is often noted that the black silk in embroideries has disintegrated and has occasionally been replaced, usually by an unsuitable yarn in an unlikely colour. The explanation given is that a metallic dye, such as iron sulphate or iron pyrites, has been used. The reason that black does not last as long as other colours is that in order to obtain a dense enough black, the yarn is boiled more than once, and this repeated boiling weakens the yarn.

In 1794 the French Government commisioned a study of the dyeing techniques in the archipelago, from where the French had imported large quantities of ready-dyed silk. The study was undertaken by Guillaume Antoine Olivier, who published his findings in his *Voyage dans l'Empire Othoman Paris*, 1801. In the second volume of that work he gives details of dyeing processes and the following recipes for certain colours:

> **light green** – boiled peach tree wood, **green** – boiled peach leaves, **dark green** – immature shells of the nut *Corylus avellana*, **rose** – boiled apple tree roots, **light pink** – boiled quince wood, **yellow** – boiled nettle tree roots, **pale yellow** – boiled broom flowers, **orange** – boiled onion skins with alum, **red** – onion skins and crushed kermes, described as the gall nut of the Holm Oak

It is not surprising that the French Government were not pleased with his findings, and had to wait until the new industrial dyes became available from Germany, sixty years later.

> Argenti gives the modern equivalents in his costume book:
> **black** – carob leaves, pomegranate rind and wood ash, or logwood, or walnut husks and iron sulphate; **blue** – washing blue with poppy seeds, or may flowers; **brown** – onion rinds or almond skins or even wine lees; **green** blackberry leaves; **orange** – wild crocus seeds; **red** –foxglove flowers (*Digitalis ferruginea*), or poppy petals; **yellow** – almond leaves, almond rind or even wild spinach, wild crocus stems and pomegranate rind.

These various descriptions show that there was a wide range of natural plants and trees used to produce a range of colours, and it would be both dogmatic and wrong to specify one particular method for dyeing any one colour.

174

15   *The Early Collectors*

The first recorded donation of a collection of Greek island embroideries was made in 1876 to the South Kensington Museum, later the Victoria and Albert Museum, by Thomas Sandwith, who had been the British Consul in Chania, Crete, from 1870 to 1885. According to his daughter, Charlotte Boys-Smith, her father had became a collector by accident. A generous man, he had given financial help both from his private and from government funds to members of the local Greek community who had suffered during the troubles that endlessly beset them in their conflict with the Turkish occupiers, and was repaid by them with gifts of embroidery and lace.

He gave 160 pieces, of which 56 were skirt panels or small covers and 100 lengths of needle and bobbin lace, to the museum, keeping only some favourite pieces for his daughter. She in turn later gave even those to the V&A Museum to complete the original donation. A few pieces were left with her daughter, the grand-daughter of the original collector, who followed the family tradition and gave the majority of what was left to the History Museum in Crete in 1977, retaining a few pieces, all of which are illustrated here.

This first collection was exhibited in January 1876, and was reviewed rather snidely in the *Saturday Review* of 22 January by a reviewer more keen on showing that he had read his Tournefort than considering the textiles themselves.

After Sandwith, most collectors were classical archaeologists working with either the Hellenic Society or the British School at Athens. Theodore Bent and William Paton, both of the Hellenic Society, had received grants to carry out various excavations: Bent received £50 in 1885 for a dig in Samos, and the same amount the following year for another in Thasos. In 1885 he published an account of his travels with his wife in the Aegean, *The Cyclades, or Life Among the Insular Greeks*, a most entertaining and not always flattering account of the islanders, which deserves to be better known. Bent portrays a real, unromantic Greece and links it, rather to its detriment, to the classical world that he was excavating. Bent also visited the Dodecanese, but sadly did not

Alan John Bayard Wace was Director of the British School in Athens from 1914 to 1923, and organised the first exhibition of Greek embroideries in 1906. He was Keeper of Textiles at the Victoria & Albert Museum from 1924 to 1934 and was very influential in promoting the study of textiles. A large number of textiles illustrated in this book were collected by him. This photograph of him in the costume of Samarina was taken when he was studying them in 1913.

175

publish an account of that visit. He collected costumes from Karpathos and Nisyros and in 1886 gave three dresses from Karpathos to the South Kensington Museum. They are acknowledged, quite rightly, as among the best examples of island embroidery in the collection. In 1914 his widow lent a further six dresses to the Burlington Fine Arts Club Exhibition: two are now in the Benaki Museum, one in Boston and a fourth one is at the Metropolitan, given by George D. Pratt in 1930.

p.80, 81

William Paton received similar grants from the the Hellenic Society for excavations in Kalymnos and elsewhere in the Dodecanese. In 1886 he gave two Kalymniote dresses to the South Kensington Museum, followed in 1902 by two pieces from a bed furnishing from Kos. Paton went on to direct the great excavation at Cnydos and was the translator of the five-volume *Greek Anthology* published by Heinemann in 1916.

In 1883 the Hellenic Society raised funds to establish a British School of Archaeology in Athens, after it had been decided not to send British archaeologists to the French School already there. It eventually opened in Athens in 1886, with F.C. Penrose as the first Director. Collecting fever passed to the new members of the School, among them Robert Carr Bosanquet, the third Director, 1900-06. He collected rather generally, and after his return to England and death, seventy of his pieces were given to the City of Newcastle University by his widow and sister-in-law in 1945. The remainder of his collection was given to the city by his son, Dr Charles Bosanquet, in 1965. The University passed the whole collection on to the Newcastle Museum, now the Tyne and Wear Museum in Newcastle, and it was exhibited at

Left Thomas Sandwith, British Consul in Chania from 1870 to 1885. He was the first collector of Cretan textiles and made the first donation of them to the South Kensington Museum in 1876. The illustrations on pages 106, 108, 110, and 113 are of pieces collected by him and still in the possession of the family. *Right* Theodore Bent, an early collector in the Aegean, who acquired most of the known examples of Karpathos pouka-misos. In 1885 he wrote an account of his travels in the Cyclades, before going to work in Ethiopia.

Richard MacGillivray Dawkins, Director of the British School in Athens 1900-6. His collection is now at the Victoria & Albert Museum. Dawkins became the first Professor of Byzantine and Modern Greek at Oxford and published two books of Greek folk tales.

the city's Laing Art Gallery in 1967. The most splendid piece in the collection is the large, complete Rhodian bed tent.

Other members of the School began to collect seriuosly, led by Richard MacGillivray Dawkins and Alan John Bayard Wace. Dawkins was Director from 1906 to1914, and travelled extensively, researching local dialects and collecting textiles in quantities that might, unkindly, be called wholesale. On his return to England he devoted himself to the study of Greek linguistics and folk tales, becoming the first Professor of Byzantine and Modern Greek at Oxford between 1920 and 1939. He lent 300 of his textiles to the Victoria and Albert Museum on permanent exhibition, then, just before his death in 1959, he gave the museum his entire collection of some 700 pieces. Although he often mentioned that he was preparing a book on his embroideries, he never did so, but contributed to articles and catalogues written by his successor at the the British School, A.J.B Wace.

Wace succeeded Dawkins in 1914, holding the post throughout the First World War and until 1923, and directed the great excavations in Mycenae. He collected avidly, both during his field work and from the dealers and the itinerant merchants that were such a feature of Athens at that time. Wace went to Greece in 1902 and must have started to collect straightaway, for as early as 1906 he organised an exhibition of 'Modern Greek Embroideries' at the Fitzwilliam Museum in Cambridge. Most of the 68 exhibits came from his and Dawkins' collections, showing how they collected together and even shared some of their finds. The catalogue contains a preface with the first analysis of the techniques, patterns and dyes used, and refers to a joint study of

these embroideries that he had made with Louisa Pesel and John L. Myres.

Louisa Pesel was Director of the Royal Hellenic School of Needlework at Athens and collected some fine pieces herself. On her return to England she wrote extensively on embroidery, and in 1920 she became the first President of the new Embroiderers' Guild, starting there the system of having portfolios of embroidery available for members to borrow and study. She led the field in writing about Greek textiles, mainly for the *Burlington Magazine*, which played such an important pioneering role in publishing textile scholarship. Her writings include contributions on 'Cretan Embroidery' (1906) and 'Aegean and Yanina Embroideries' (1907).

In 1914 The Burlington Fine Arts Club (BFAC) held a large exhibition entitled 'Old Embroideries of the Greek Islands and Turkey'. For the first time domestic peasant embroidery was shown to be worthy of collecting, alongside ivories, Italian maiolica and English earthenware, for all of which earlier exhibitions had been held by the Burlington. The exhibition contained 192 pieces, of which only 20 were not Greek. Dawkins lent 71 of these and Wace 31, accounting for more than half of the total display. Wace's introduction to the exhibition catalogue set out information based on his own and on Dawkins' research. He established the glossary that is still in use today and the

The Burlington Fine Arts Club Exhibition of 1914. Case B *above* contained doors, panels and valances from Dodecanese bed tents. Case A *right* contained bed covers from the Ionian Islands, also bolster and cushion covers.

attributions he made then are mostly accepted even now. The exhibition was a landmark in the study of the textiles, introducing them to a new, wider public. Wace and Dawkins followed the exhibition with two articles in the *Burlington Magazine* in which the houses and the environment in which the embroideries were made are discussed.

In 1919 Wace gave 62 pieces to the Victoria and Albert Museum, where five years later he was appointed successor to A.F. Kendrick as Keeper of Textiles, remaining in the post until 1934. In 1925 he sold 90 pieces from his collection to George Hewitt Myers who had founded the Textile Museum in Washington DC that same year. Myers had been collecting since 1910 and after his purchase from Wace was able to endow the museum with the finest collection of Greek textiles anywhere at that time. It was exhibited in 1928, and Wace wrote the catalogue. The collection is admirably described and illustrated in James Trilling's *Aegean Crossroads*, 1983.

During Wace's keepership he established himself as an authority on textiles and extended his interest to cover a very large field, publishing articles in journals on both sides of the Atlantic. He continued to collect and to advise other collectors, and among these was Beatrice Lindell Cook, who had inherited a collection of textiles from her husband, Frank, the son of Thomas Cook of Cook's Tours. Frank was

the family representative in Egypt, where he made the majority of his purchases. After his death Mrs Cook asked Wace to study the collection, and in 1935, when he had become Professor of Classical Archaeology at Cambridge, he published 500 copies of *Mediterranean and Near Eastern Embroideries from the Collection of Mrs. F.H. Cook*, which includes 120 examples, 64 of which are Greek. The book remains the standard work on the subject, and the splendid illustrations, many of which are in excellent colour, have been a vital reference for collectors ever since. In her introductory note Mrs Cook says that all the textiles were collected by her husband in the 1880s – a kind gesture since we now know that she continued buying right up to the publication of the book. Wace directed her to fine pieces that he saw on the London market, and she paid 250 and 350 guineas for Yanina and Rhodian pieces from Liberty's while Wace was paying 4 shillings for a Naxos piece from Waring and Gillow.

Beatrice Cook bought very widely and was extremely generous in her donations. In 1946 she donated 9 splendid Turkish velvets to the Fitzwilliam Museum, which were shown in Vienna at the 'Die Turken vor Wien' exhibition in 1983. She was also willing to sell pieces to other collectors, who were delighted to have examples from a collection which was, because of the book, considered to be the most prestigious private collection. The balance of the Cook Collection was given to the Saint Louis Art Museum in stages: 3 pieces in 1951, 69 in

Three Cretan skirts were displayed in this case. The middle one, dated 1757, is in the Victoria & Albert Museum, the other two are illustrated on pages 2, 106 and 113. The other dresses are from Rhodes and mainland Greece.

180

This case contained pieces from the Sporades, the Northern Islands and one piece from Epirus. The middle bolster in the bottom row is shown on page 93, the small cushion on page 86, the Samos strip on page 105 and the Epirus strip on page 137.

1952 and 28 in 1955. The museum exhibited the collection in March 1953; Wace attended the show and gave a lecture at the opening. The museum still has 63 of these 100 pieces, the rest having been de-accessioned by auction.

Wace went in 1943 as Professor of Archaeology and Classics to Alexandria, where he met Baron George de Menasce, a collector of Islamic art. Wace introduced him to the Greek textiles that were being brought into Egypt at that time by refugees from Greece. De Menasce amassed a large collection of Greek and Ottoman pieces and, at Wace's instigation, he donated 169 pieces, of which 50 are Greek, to the Fitzwilliam between 1946 and 1950, including three Turkish pieces that he had bought from Mrs Cook.

In 1956 Wace lent 200 of his Greek textiles and 37 others to the Liverpool Museum, and these were exhibited in the Lower Horseshoe

Gallery accompanied by a fine catalogue prepared by Elaine Tankard, the Keeper of Textiles, from notes that Wace had prepared. Wace later sold his entire collection of 309 pieces for £3000 to the museum, which used part of its War Damage Grant to pay for it. The sale included the 200 pieces previously lent, plus Skyros and Naxos pieces, 32 costumes and two sets of rather coarse jewellery from Astypalaia, the *armatossia*, which had been displayed at the BFAC with one of the Bent Astypalaian dresses. A large number of pieces from this collection are illustrated in this book.

H.J.W.Tillyard, J.L.Myres, and Augustus Daniel were at Athens during Bosanquet's and Dawkins' time, and all collected. Tillyard became an authority on Byzantine music and was later Master of Jesus College, Cambridge. His collection of 22 pieces, including 3 that he had bought from Mrs Cook, was given to the Whitworth Art Gallery in Manchester in 1968. They had been shown at the Exhibition of Greek Art that was held at the Royal Academy in 1946 as a memorial to those who had died in the Second World War 'for the cause of Liberty in Greece and the Greek Seas'. In the exhibition, which covered all Greek art, 54 pieces of embroidery were shown which belonged to collectors other than Dawkins and Wace.

J.L.Myres, who was subsequently knighted, was an official of the Hellenic Society, and at an early date was appointed the Society's Keeper of Photographs. He became a classical geographer and was a member of the Commission on the Dodecanese during the 1914-18 war. His collection of 52 textiles was given by his widow to the Ashmolean Museum in Oxford in 1960.

Sir Augustus Daniel's collection of 44 items was given to the Fitzwilliam Museum in 1949, and included 26 pieces of Greek island work of a very high quality, 5 having been shown at the BFAC in 1914. There is now no trace of the collections made by other archaeologists from Athens, such as Guy Dickins, Rev. William MacGregor and Clarke Thornhill.

The collecting tradition continued in Athens long after the first feverish surge had passed. In 1934 John Buxton, then an undergraduate at New College, Oxford, joined the British School at Athens and collected embroideries both on the mainland and in the islands. He gave 19 pieces of his collection to the Ashmolean in 1977, and their quality shows that it was still possible to buy interesting pieces in the 1930s.

Apart from Frank Cook, the only serious English collectors who were not Greek archaeologists were Percy Newberry, an Egyptologist, Sir Arthur Church, a scientist, and Sir William Lawrence, a chemist. Professor Newberry had worked in Egypt from 1890, first with Flinders Petrie in the Fayoum and then in 1923 with Howard Carter in Luxor and on the Tutankhamun discovery. He was Brunner Professor of Archaeology at Liverpool, and between 1929 and 1932 was Professor of Ancient History and Archaeology at Cairo University. His primary textile interest was classical Egypt and early Islam, and he formed an admirable collection of Fatimid and Mamluk textiles and early printed Indian cloths that were found in association with Islamic burials in Egypt. He gave this collection to the Ashmolean in 1946, and gave his other collection, the one he called 'modern decorative', to the Whitworth in 1949. This modern collection consists of 400 pieces, 100 of which are Greek, 100 are Turkish and the remainder are Mediterranean and European.

Professor Newberry's wife, Essie, was an accomplished needlewoman herself and some of her exemplary fine stitchwork is still on show at the V&A Museum. She was involved in the Embroiderers' Guild and served as Vice President 1922-45 and Honorary Treasurer 1935-8. She also contributed an article, 'Stitchery' with Louisa Pesel, to 'A Book of Old Embroidery' for a special number of the *Studio Magazine* in 1921. This illustrated a large number of Greek pieces in both their collections, all today at the Whitworth. She also published articles in *Embroidery*, the journal of the Embroiderers' Guild, on Egyptian and Moroccan textiles, drawing on her own collection. One suspects that she was the driving force behind the wide range of the Newberry Collection.

Sir William Lawrence collected some Greek textiles, although he was mainly interested in Turkish work, and wrote the short introduction to the Turkish section in the 1914 BFAC catalogue. Sir Arthur Church, a metallurgist who donated a large number of Japanese sword furnishings to the V&A, also collected textiles widely and after his death in 1915 his widow offered 13 Greek textiles, 9 of which had been displayed at the BFAC in 1914, to the museum. These pieces had been offered for a charity sale at Christie's in aid of the Red Cross in 1916, but at the request of the V&A were withdrawn and were finally given to the museum. They are of considerable interest, particularly the three fine Cretan skirt pieces.

The collection of about 50 pieces at the Royal Scottish Museum in Edinburgh was made between 1892 and 1974. They were mainly donations and a few purchases, the main donors being Mrs Ionides and her family. The collection includes the three most splendid pieces of Epirus embroidery described earlier.

These are the principal British collections, formed principally on the basis of donations made by the major collectors, who were also influential in the creation of the two major American collections - that of Myers at Washington and the Cook Collection in Saint Louis. Other important North American collections are in Boston, Chicago, California and Honolulu and, of course, at the Metropolitan Museum in New York and the Royal Ontario Museum in Canada.

The Boston Museum of Fine Arts has a very large and diverse textile collection, begun by Martin Brimmer with his donation of some wonderful Turkish velvets in 1877, and continued with many other bequests. These include that of Denman Waldo Ross and the large gift from Elizabeth Day McCormick made in 1943. The collection was recently published in *Greek Island Embroideries* by Susan L. MacMillan.

Burton Yost Berry, who lived for many years in Turkey and the Balkans, made collections in various areas of the minor arts, from Hellenistic jewellery to Ottoman door furnishings and Turkish *ebru* paper. He gave his collection of Greek and Turkish textiles to the Art Institute of Chicago, which now has a collection of some 80 Greek island pieces, 64 of which were part of the Berry Donation. He wrote about his collection in *Embroidery* in 1936, and in the *Boston Arts Bulletin* in 1932 and 1938, mainly about his Turkish pieces. I have found nothing that he specifically wrote on Greek work, and I assume that he considered the many Yanina pieces that he owned to be Turkish, as was the fashion at that time. The collection was published, with very fine illustrations, as *Turkish and Greek Island Embroideries* by Margaret Gentles in 1964.

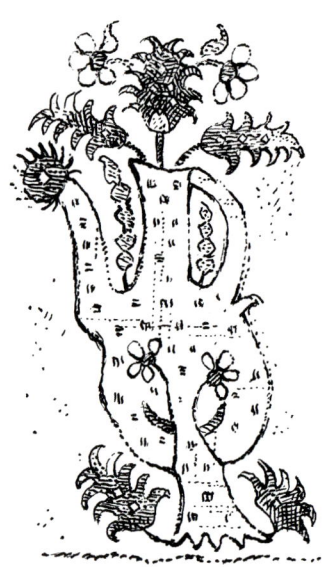

Henrietta Foster Brewer of Oakland, California, followed the tradition of the archaeologist collector. She was a descendent of the Josiah Brewer who ran the Independent American Mission in Smyrna in 1810. After studying at Berkeley and graduating from there in 1895, she went to Greece and Turkey to carry out field work. She collected quite extensively during her time there and eventually her very large and varied collection of about 700 pieces was distributed by her family to institutions with which she had had close connections. In 1933 her sister, Mrs Fowler, donated 120 pieces to the Honolulu Academy of Arts in her memory, to complement the Academy's considerable holdings of Oriental textiles. Another 115 pieces were given to the Mills College Gallery in Oakland in 1943, and were exhibited there in November of that year. A further 322 pieces were given to the Lowie Museum of Anthropology in Berkeley, of which about 160 are described as Greek, from both the islands and the mainland. This collection was used for many years as part of the teaching collection of the University of California. Her niece, Mrs Van S. Merle-Smith, gave a further collection of Greek textiles and costumes to the Metropolitan Museum of Art, New York in 1941 and 1953.

The Metropolitan has a large textile collection, including a Textile Study Collection with about 137 Greek pieces from a number of bequests. The Friedrich Fischbach Collection of 26 pieces was purchased in 1909, and Richard B. Seager, who had been an archaeologist with the American School in Athens and a friend of both Wace and Sir Arthur Evans, the excavator of Knossos, donated his collection of 49 pieces in 1926. The Michael J. Friedsam collection was given in 1931, that of George D. Pratt in 1930 and 1932, and the George and Mary Monk Gift in 1957. The collection covers the islands, especially Crete, and includes 29 embroidered chemises, mainly donated from the Henrietta Brewer collection, which have been studied by Dr Linda Welters and published in the *Bulletin of the Needle and Bobbin Club*. The Metropolitan held an exhibition of Greek island embroideries in 1943 with the Greek War Relief Association, when many of the these textiles were shown for the first, and only, time.

The Cincinnati Art Museum held an exhibition of Greek island embroideries in 1931, drawn from the collections of two Cincinnati citizens, Mrs Lucien Wulsin and Dr Carl Blegen. The collection of Dr Blegen was given to the museum in 1976.

The Royal Ontario Museum in Toronto has 126 Greek embroideries, of which 79 are from the islands, mainly from purchases and two major donations: Lillian Massey Treble in 1910 and 1912, and Jean Alexander in 1972, who gave the museum her father's collection.

The main European collection is, as one would expect, in Athens at the Benaki Museum. It contains 940 embroideries and 296 costumes, and unlike any other museum all the pieces are admirably displayed. The majority of the items were collected by Antony Benaki when he lived in Alexandria. He returned to Greece in 1926 and on the death of his father, Emmanuel, he converted the family mansion to a private museum to house the collection. In 1931 the museum was donated to the Greek nation with all the contents. It now also contains the various donations made by the other members of the Benaki family, as well as 385 pieces donated by Mrs Helen Stathatos between 1949 and 1975. Benaki's main interest was Islamic art, and the museum has some 2300 Coptic and Islamic textiles. In the great Moslem Art Exhibition held in Alexandria in 1925 over a third of the total number of exhibits came from Antony Benaki's private collection, indicating the quality and size of his original collection. The other museums that have important holdings of textiles are the Museum of Greek Folk Art and the Historic Museum in Athens and the History Museum in Chania in Crete.

Also of importance is the collection at the Iparmúvészeti Múzeum in Budapest, composed of 346 pieces of which 257 are Turkish and 44 Greek. However, a number of pieces, such as those from Epirus and Yanina, which are today classified as Greek, are there called Turkish. The oldest pieces, some 31 of the Turkish pieces, which are mainly seventeenth-century horse trappings such as saddles and blankets, come from the old Esterházy collection acquired by the museum in 1949. Other donations came from the collection of Dr Otto Fettick and from the National Exhibitions of 1885 and 1886. The late Károly Gombos organised an exhibition of the textiles at the Castle Museum of Nagytétényi in 1981, with a small illustrated catalogue. The museum has instituted a three year study program of the Esterházy Collection, which will provide new information on how the pieces were collected.

The Danish Decorative Arts Museum in Copenhagen has a small collection of 80 pieces, mainly collected by Erik Lassen in Athens in 1960-1. Others were purchased from Soustiel in Paris after the 1963 Copenhagen Exhibition organised by Rigmor Krarup, for which a small catalogue was published.

The Museum for Decorative Arts in Dresden has some 36 Greek embroideries among its 12,000 textile items. All of them were purchased from dealers in Paris and Istanbul between the years 1878 and 1887. The collection was illustrated in a small volume published in 1986 in Leipzig, with a commentary by Ursula Hennig. The book is interesting in that it preserves the tradition of the late nineteenth

century, identifying all Greek pieces as either Rhodes or Yanina. The first 24 pieces, which are clearly all from Naxos, are described as Rhodian, as are a number of Koan pieces. Turkish pieces are described as Persian and Caucasian ones as Turkish, and a quite untenable relationship is drawn between Rhodian and Moroccan stitches.

The Musée du Tissus in Lyon specialises in woven fabrics but also has an admirable collection of other textiles, among which there are two spectacular Ionian cushion covers. They are both in the drawn thread technique and were bought in 1875, sewn together as a carpet, from a visting Italian textile dealer for 60 francs, a large sum at the time. This is the first recorded purchase of a Greek island textile that I have been able to find in any museum.

There are other small holdings in museums all over the world, demonstrating the interest that these embroideries have aroused and how they are now treated as art objects, far removed from their insular peasant beginnings.

Bibliography

Textiles

Argenti, Philip, *Costumes of Chios, 15th -20th Century*. London 1953.

Bellinger, Louise, 'Cretan Embroideries in the Textile Museum, Washington', *Cretan Chronicles*. Kalokairinos, Heracleion 1950

Currey, C. Maisie, 'Embroideries of the Greek Islands', *Embroidery* Vol. 1 No. 2 & 3 1950

Erber, Christian, *A Wealth of Silk and Velvet*. Edition Temmen. Bremen. 1993

Frangaki, Evangelias, *The Folk Art of Crete. Weaving and Dyeing*. Athens. 1974

Geijer, A., *Oriental Textiles in Sweden*. Copenhagen 1951

Gerola, Giuseppe, *I Costumi Muliebri nelle Tredici Sporadi*. Emporium Vol. 37

Gervers, V., *Influence of Ottoman Turkish Textiles and Costume in Eastern Europe*. Royal Ontario Museum 1982

Hatzimichaili, Angelika, *Greek Popular Art I. Skyros,* Makris, Athens 1925

— *Examples of Greek Decoration*. Pyrsos SA, Athens 1929

— *Greek Popular Art 2. Roumlouki, Trikeri, Ikaria*. Pyrsos SA, Athens 1931

— *Vilia on Cithareona*. Athens 1933

— *Middle Eastern Embroideries. A critique on Wace*. Yanina 1935

— *Greek Embroidery. Epirus, Skyros*. Byzantisch-Neu Griechische Jahrbücher, Vol 18

Hauser, Walter, *Greek Island Embroideries*, Greek War Relief Association, New York 1943

Heichelheim, F.M., 'Silk Trade and Silk Industry in Byzantium', *Ciba Review* 75.

Ioannou-Yannara, T., *Greek Threadwork Lace*, Melissa Publishing, Athens 1989

— *Greek Bobbin Lace*, Melissa Publishing, Athens 1990

Johnstone, Pauline, *Greek Island Embroidery*. London 1961

— *The Byzantine Tradition in Church Embroidery*. London 1967

Kendrick, A.F., *Catalogue of Textiles from Burying Grounds in Egypt. Vol. 1 Graeco Roman, Vol. 2 Transition, Vol. 3 Coptic*. V&A Museum, London 1920-22

— *Catalogue of Muhammadan Textiles of the Medieval Period*. V&A Museum, 1924

— *Catalogue of Early Medieval Woven Fabrics*. V&A Museum, London 1925

Koutsika Collection, *Engravings of Chios, Vol. 1 Costume, Vol. 2 Maps*. Aipos Series No. 14

Kühnel, Ernst, *Islamische Stoffe aus Ägyptischen Gräbern*. Berlin 1927

Lamm, Carl Johan, *Some Mamluk Embroideries*.

— *Cotton in Medieval Textiles of the Near East*. Paris 1937

Lopez, Roberto S., 'The Silk Industry in the Byzantine Empire' *Speculum* Vol. XX Jan. 1945

Marzouk, M.A., *History of Textile Industry in Alexandria*. Alexandria University 1955

Monte Santo, Marica, *L'Isola dei Gigli*. Ministero delle Colonie Vol. 7

— *La Città Sacra*. Ministero delle Colonie Vol. 12

— 'Il Ricamo nelle Sporadi' *Dedalo* XI 1930-31

— *Illustrazione Italiana* LX 1933

Pesel, Louisa, 'The Embroideries of the Aegean', *Burlington Magazine* Vol. X 1907 p. 230 ff.

— 'Cretan Embroideries', *Burlington Magazine* Vol. X 1906 p. 155 ff.

— 'So-called' Yanina Embroideries', *Burlington Magazine* Vol. X 1907 p. 32 ff.

— *Stitches from Eastern Embroideries. Portfolio* No. 2. London 1914.

— 'A Book of Old Embroidery', *The Studio* 1921

Pfister, R., *Textiles de Palmyre*. Paris 1934

— 'Matériaux pour servir au classement des Textiles Egyptiens postérieurs à la Conquête Arabe', *Revue Arts Asiatiques* X 1

Stathatos, Hélène, *Collection - Les Objets Byzantins et Post-Byzantins*. Limoges 1957

Tarsouli, A., *Costumes Grecs*. Athens 1941

— *Embroideries and Costumes of the Dodecanese*. Athens 1951

Taylor, R.R., 'The Early Collectors', *Hali* Vol. 36 Oct 1987

— *Ottoman Embroidery*. London 1993

— 'Greece, the Greek Islands and Albania', *5000 Years of Textiles* (Ed Jennifer Harris). British Museum, London 1993

BIBLIOGRAPHY

Wace, A.J.B., *Catalogue of Modern Greek Embroideries*. Fitzwilliam Museum, Cambridge 1905
— *Catalogue of a Collection of Old Embroideries of the Greek Islands and Turkey*. Burlington Fine Arts Club, London 1914
— *Mediterranean and Near East Embroideries from the Collection of Mrs F.H.Cook*. Halton & Co, London 1935
— 'Weaving or Embroidery', *American Journal of Archaeology* Vol. LII No.I 1948
— & R.M. Dawkins, 'Greek Embroideries 1', 'Greek Embroideries 2', *Burlington Magazine* Vol. 26 1914
Welters, L., 'Embroidery on Greek Women's Chemises in the Metropolitan Museum of Art'. *Bulletin of the Needle and Bobbin Club*, Vol. 67, No. 142 1984
— 'Greek Women's Chemises', *Dress*, Vol. 8 1982
Zervos, S.G., *Rhodes, Capitale du Dodécanèse*. Paris 1920. Illustrations of Rhodian textiles in J.N.Catsoulis Collection.
Zora, P., *Embroidery and Jewellery of Greek National Costumes*. Athens 1966

Museum Publications

Athens
Benaki Museum. *Guide* 1936 and 1986; *Hellenic National Costumes*, Vol. I 1948, Vol. II 1954; *Greek Folk Costume* (Angelika Hatzimichaili), Melissa 2 Vols 1977, 1983; *Skyros Embroideries* 1965; *Crete-Dodecanese-Cyclades Embroideries* 1966; *Greek Embroideries* (H. Polychroniadis) 1980
Museum of Greek Folk Art. *Catalogue* 1977
Historical and Ethnological Society of Greece. *Greek Embroidery* 1993
— *Greek Costumes* 1993

Skyros
Faltaïts Museum. *Ta Skyriana Tsemberakia* (Anastasias Faltaïts). Athens 1985

Boston
Museum of Fine Arts. *Greek Island Embroideries* (Susan L. MacMillan)

Chicago
Chicago Art Institute. *Turkish and Greek Island Embroideries*, including the Burton Yost Berry Collection (Margaret Gentles) 1964

Cincinnati
Cincinnati Art Museum. 'Embroideries of the Aegean Islands' (G.L. McCann). *Bulletin* Vol. II No. 2 April 1931
— *Exhibition* Winter 1931

Dresden
Dresden Staatsliche Kunstsammlung *Rhodos Stickereien* (Ursula Hennig). Verlag für die Frau 1986

Honolulu
Academy of Arts. *A Festival of Flowers* 1977

London
Victoria and Albert Museum. *A Guide to Greek Island Embroidery* (Pauline Johnstone) 1972

Liverpool
Liverpool Public Museums. *An Exhibition of Mediterranean Embroideries from Professor Alan J.B.Wace* (Elaine Tankard) 1956

New York
Metropolitan Museum of Art. 'Greek Island Embroideries' (Walter Hauser) *Bulletin*, Vol. 1 1943, pp.254-60

St Gallen
Industrie und Gewerbe Museum. *Catalogue* (Leopold Iklé) Textil Sammlung 1908

Washington
The Textile Museum. *Aegean Crossroads* (James Trilling) 1983

Glossary

akopti an incomplete dowry dress, with uncut neck.

aloni The inner courtyard of a Skyriote house.

aratzidelles Narrow ribbons of needle lace or crochetting made in imitation of reticella lace.

armatossia Set of festive jewellery worn by Astypalaian women.

aspitha A mythological figure, half-woman half-animal or half-woman half-snake.

bakaleto A counterpane or bed tidy. Corfu.

baqqam A dark wood producing black or dark red dye.

bebilla A strip of needle lace, crochet or tatting used as a decorative edging.

bolme The centre post and balustrade holding up the balcony housing the sofa or bed. Skyros.

bombyx The silkworm or its coccon.

bradyfyllo (also spathofyllo, platyfyllo) The broad-leaf pattern composed or two leaves set opposite each other. This is the pattern arbitrarily called the 'king pattern'.

cariola A spare, small bed in Cycladic houses.

cevre, tsevredes Square head scarf or shawl

chrysomandilo An embroidered scarf incorporating gold or silver strip worn by women at Astypalaian festivals.

colletti A shawl made of embroidered pieces joined by strips of lace. Crete.

derzidhes Profesional tailors making court or civil uniforms. Epirus.

dilinia Large sea-going vessels, ships 'of the line'. Skyros and Astypalaia.

dixos A medallion pattern like a 'gul'. Dodecanese.

embolia, bolia A long scarf or sash embroidered at both ends. Skyros and Epirus, Siphnos, Kythnos.

fylfot A four-footed pattern, like a swastika but lying in either direction.

gasmouli The children of mixed marriages between Frankish men and local women.

gazi A stitch or stitching, or even the hem of a garment.

glastron A vase pattern. Dodecanese.

goletta A sailing vessel. Skyros.

gomlek A shirt of fine cotton or of a crimped weave. Skyros.

gorgon A mermaid. Crete and Skyros.

gossypium The genus of cotton-bearing plants.

gouna A short waistcoat worn by women, usually fur-trimmed.

grafta A group of stitches based on a drawn pattern.

gul A medallion found in Central Asian and Turkish carpets. See 'dixos'.

gynacea The women's quarters in Byzantine Palaces. Traditionally where the first silk looms were set up.

Janissary The new Ottoman army, mainly composed of youths captured within the empire.

jijim A hand weave, with weft embroidery.

kalimeres Good Day, a small embroidery from Chios.

kalimkar Pen work, a printed cloth. Chios.

kambur A hunch-backed pattern, a curved branch.

karavi A sailing boat pattern.

kazzazidhes Silk spinners. Epirus.

kentima The common word for embroidery.

kormi The skirt of a poukamiso with embroidery at the hem.

kortina The common word for a bed curtain or a hanging.

koumbaros Brother-in-law or close relative, 'compadre'.

koumpaso The area above the door in island bed tents, usually filled with heraldic and other designs, also known as 'mostra'.

lales A tulip, any flower pattern.

Mahona The guild of Genoese merchants who ran Chios.

makrama A woven or embroidered hand cloth.

metrita Those stitches which are formed by counting the threads in the base weave.

milosperveri The octagonal plate set in a ceiling from which the Rhodian bed tent hung.

mostra A display, used to describe the patterns above the gable of a bed-tent door. Dodecanese

mouseion The same as 'mostra'.

mussandires A cupboard, Turkish. Sporades.

nakshe A drawn pattern, usually from Iran.

pankos A box or stool placed alongside a bed, parapankos, to act as a step.

panomustachia A shawl or headcloth drawn tightly around the mouth.

perdikes Partridges. Aegean and Ionian pattern.

peripetasmata Curtains or room dividers in houses of the classic period.

phrygium opus Embroidery in cross stitch or using metal thread, wire or strip.

platyfyllo See 'bradyfyllo'

ploumi A pattern or design in the islands.

ploumizo To decorate with a pattern, usually in embroidery.

plumarium opus Embroidery in long stitch, like a feather.

poikillein To weave or embroider with colours.

portolano An illustrated chart showing harbours, wind directions and distances.

poukamiso A woman's shift, worn singly or in layers. Usually embroidered at the hem, on the sleeves and at the neck.

risha A feather, the word for embroidery patterns. Arabic.

qadi A judge, leader of the community. Turkish.

sendonia A large sheet or counterpane.

skleta Woman's skirt. Dodecanese.

skolopendra A centipede pattern. Dodecanese costume.

skoufia A cap or bonnet.

skouta A skirt border embroidered with isolated patterns. Sporades.

spathofyllo See 'bradyfyllo'

spitha A design based on a 'spark', lines radiating upwards.

staphylato A pattern like a bunch of grapes.

stithopano A cloth used to cover the breasts. Chios.

tavlomantilo A table cloth. Sporades.

trachilia Embroidered neck opening on a poukamiso.

tsemberakia Child's embroidered head cloth. Skyros.

tsevredes A scarf - Turkish cevre.

vagioli A table runner. Sporades.

xombli A sampler, Latin *exemplum*. Dodecanese.

xouna A witch.

yastik A bolster. Turkish.

zatouni A costume style from Astypalaia.

Index

Photograph credits

I would like to thank and acknowledge all those who have kindly lent me photographs for the book: Art Institute, Chicago 153; Benaki Museum, Athens 10, 20, 81, 97, 112, 118, 122, 155; Christie's, South Kensington Ltd, London 58; Fitzwilliam Museum, Cambridge 86, 93, 95, 156; Joss Graham, London 80; Iparmuveszeti Museum, Budapest 48 (c,d), 49 (a,b,c), 145, 151; Liverpool Museum, Liverpool 5, 9, 13, 17, 21, 32, 33, 37, 43, 44, 45, 48 (b), 49 (d), 50, 51, 53, 54, 55 (b), 61, 67, 69, 77, 78, 83, 85 (a), 94, 96, 100, 102, 104, 105, 109, 114, 125, 140, 148, 152, 159, 160, 168, 170, 171, 174; Museum of International Folk Art, Santa Fe 126; Phillips Fine Art Auctioneers, London 6, 90, 103, 129, 130, 143, 166; Royal Scottish Museum, Edinburgh 138, 139; Textile Arts, New York 132; Tyne & Wear Museums, Newcastle upon Tyne 60; Whitworth Art Gallery, Manchester 39, 144. Private collectors: 2, 23, 28, 79, 106, 108, 110, 113, 137; Author's collection: 18, 24, 30, 41, 48 (a), 55 (a), 56, 62, 63, 66, 73, 82, 84, 85 (b), 111, 116, 117, 121, 133, 135, 141, 146, 165, 176, 177, 178, 179, 180, 181. I would like to thank Elizabeth Vickers, Clive Loveless, Tony Birks-Hay and Antony Maitland for taking some of the photographs and helping in obtaining them from various sources.

192

The Plague at Rhodes

And who knows how to tell us of all their arts
* and of the beautiful things their little hands made,*
Patterned and broad leaf work, sewn with skill and craft
* on fine linen, all types of designs set in order,*
Which they enriched with silver and gold,
* with all the arts of the Muses like good painters.*
Bedtents, cushions, curtains and kerchiefs,
* worked with quinces, roses, vine tendrils and grapes,*
Flowers, pomegranates and myrtle, flowers of every kind.
* They embroidered them with feeling, with happiness and song.*
I tell you, if any one had been there to look carefully
* at the handicraft they worked on, they would have praised it.*

Emmanuel Georgillas, 1485